Follow Your Heart
and
Free Your Mind

an Art Journal by:
Kristen Collins

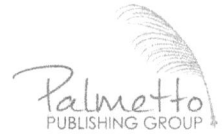

Palmetto Publishing Group, LLC
Charleston, SC

Quantity sales are available on quantity purchases.
For details email the publisher at: Info@PalmettoPublishingGroup.com.

ISBN-13: 978-1-944313-19-7
ISBN-10: 1-944313-19-2

To my Husband, thank you for standing by me and being my rock and best friend in this new exciting path of our life. I love you always and forever.

To my Dad and G-ma, always pushing and supporting me in any decisions throughout my life. Y'all are awesome and I love y'all.

To all my fellow Lupus Warriors, never give up the fight. Stay strong and fight on.

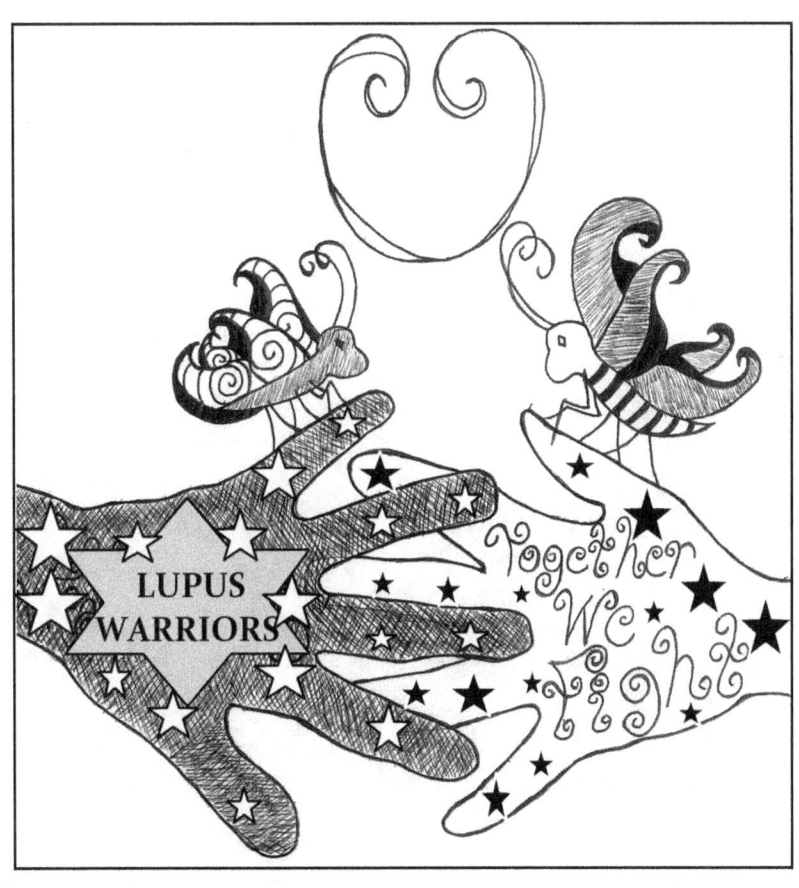

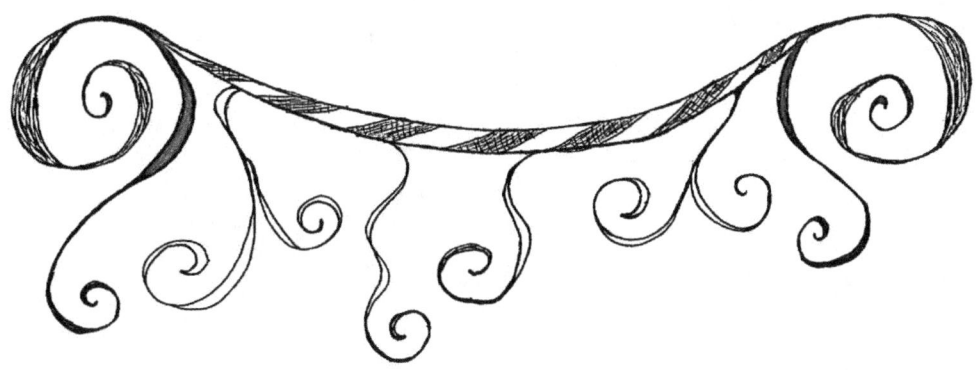

Follow Your Heart and Free Your Mind

I developed an art journal out of the many creations that poured out of my imagination and onto paper. They flowed so fast that often I would find myself drawing all day and into the night. It was exhilarating!

I've created this journal to be cross generational because artists come in all ages, cultures and stages in life. From the very young child to the great grandmother, this journal is designed to help bring out the artist in everyone.

I'm a woman who has struggled with Lupus most of my life, but I've also been blessed to have a wonderful husband and three rambunctious kiddos. I've strived to find a purpose in life that will reach out to others and offer them something positive in life. I wanted to show my children that even in the midst of difficulty, a person can have what they want in life. All it takes is a dream, hard work and dedication.

So why did I decide to dedicate myself to the creation of an ART journal?

Art Journals are a great way to express yourself. Sometimes the artist works with words by writing amazing stories, recording memories, expressing feelings, or just keeping a private diary. But sometimes it's through pictures. Drawing, doodling, painting, or coloring. The artist doesn't have to be limited and I like that idea.

I hope you are inspired to add to my drawings and create some new ones for yourself!

Enjoy!

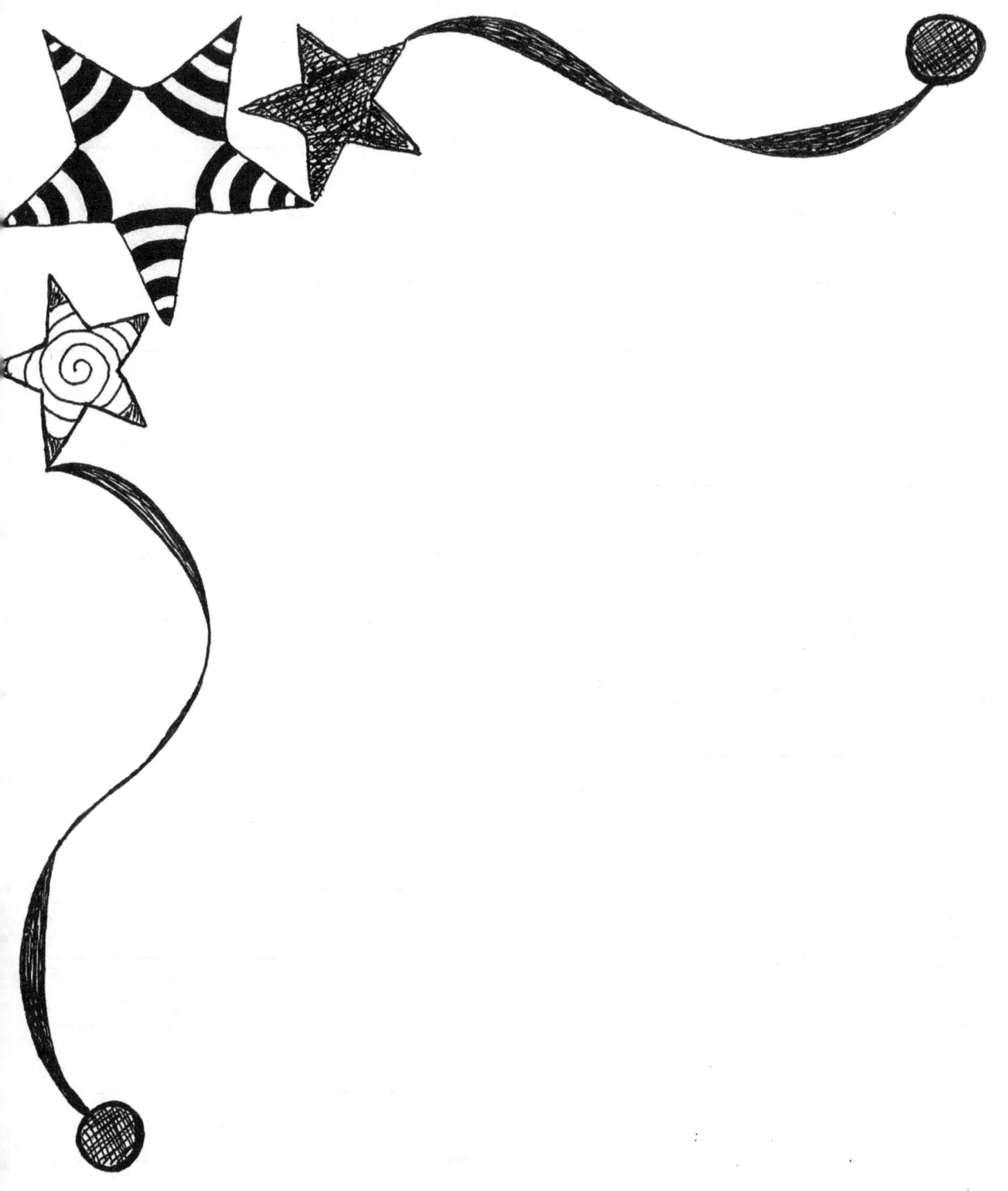

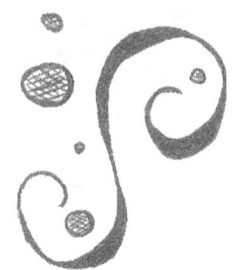
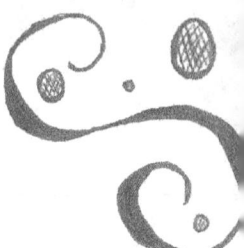

4

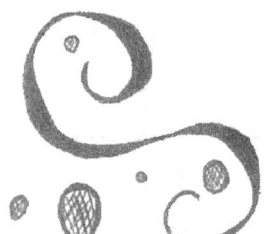
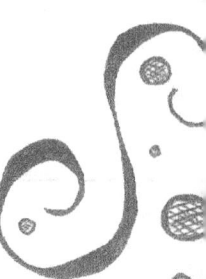

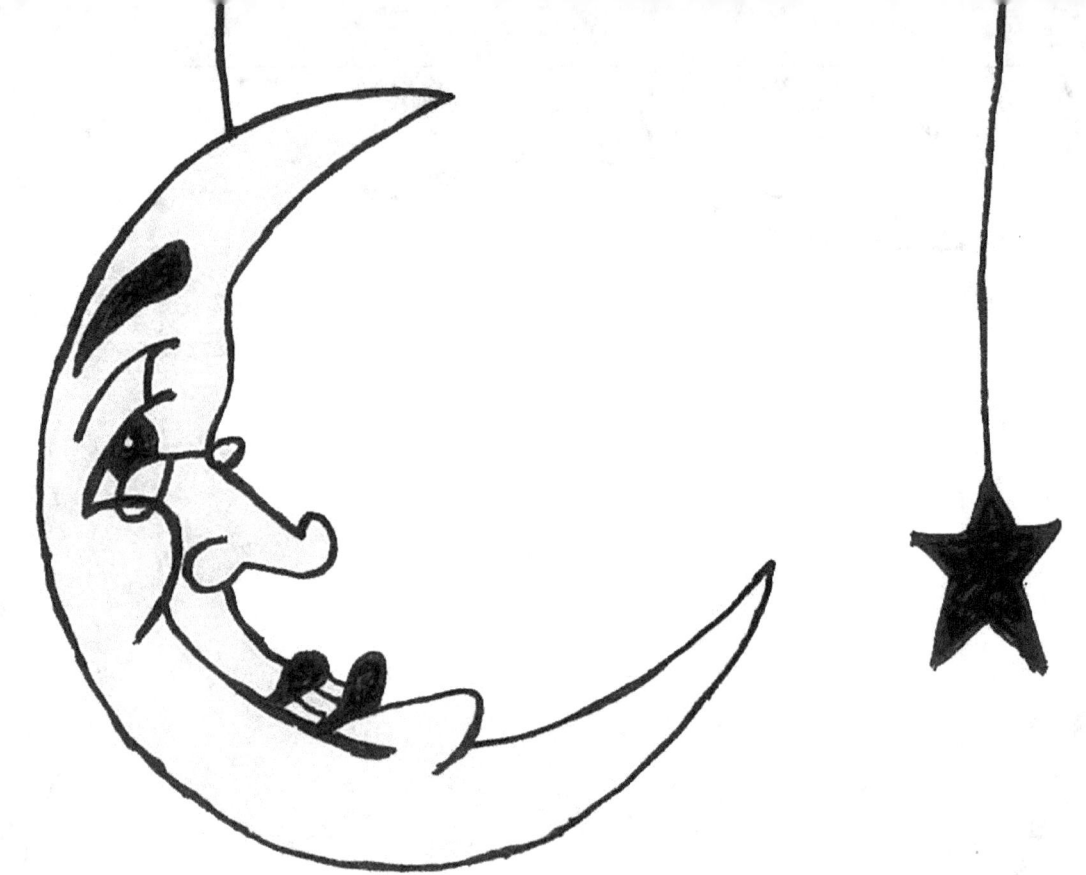

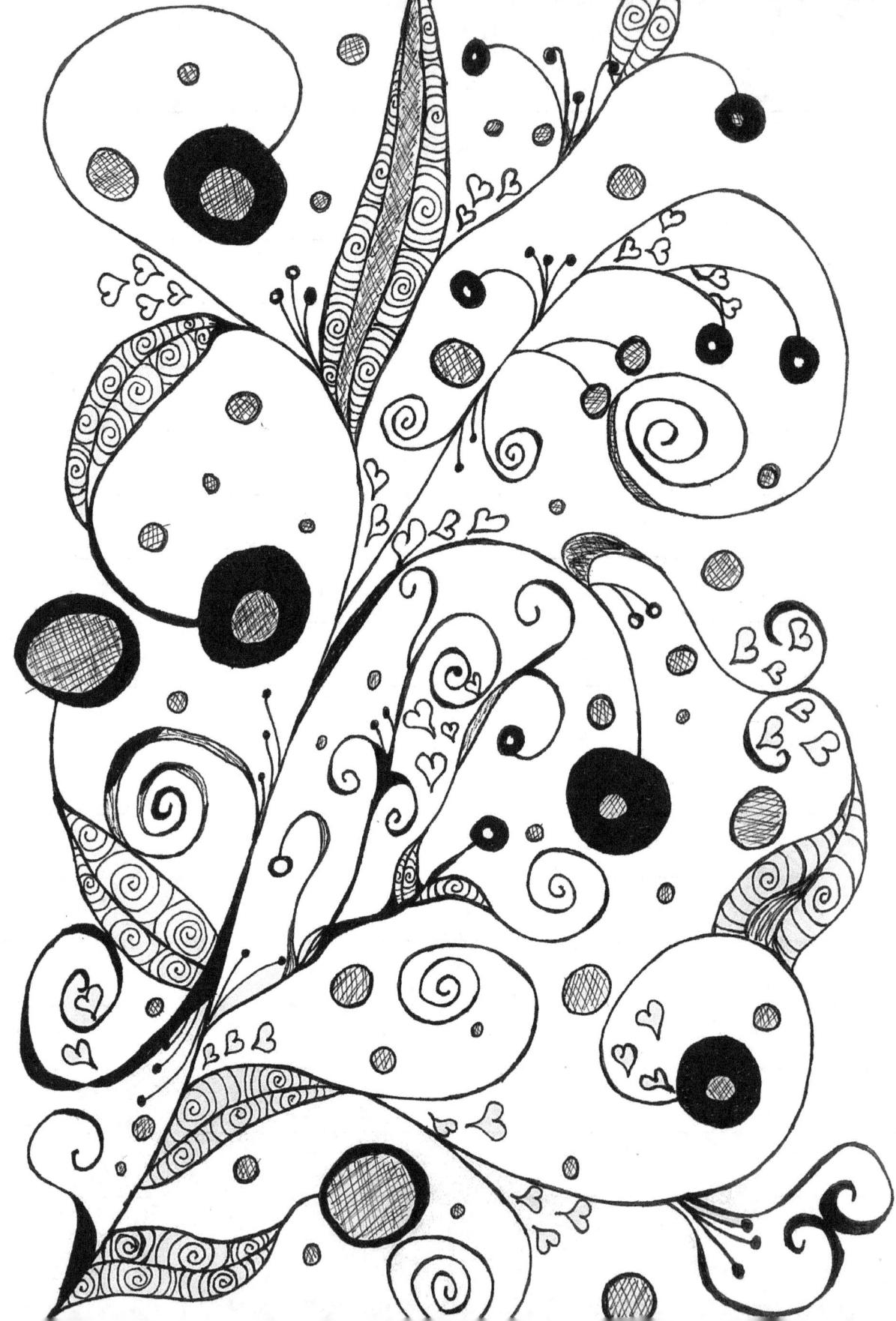

"Why, sometimes I've believed as many as six impossible things before breakfast."

-The Queen,
Through the Looking-Glass, and What Alice Found There,
by Lewis Carroll

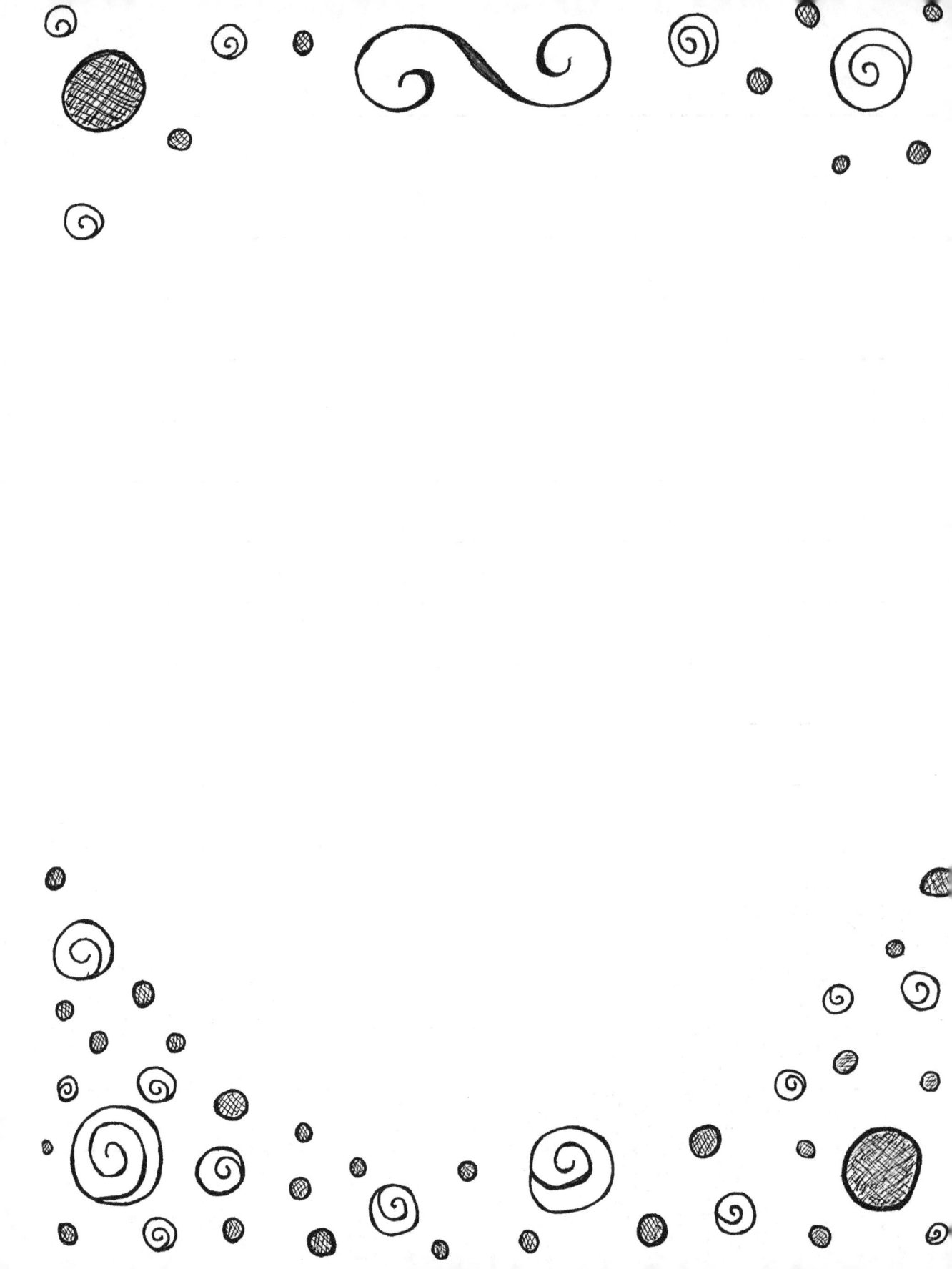

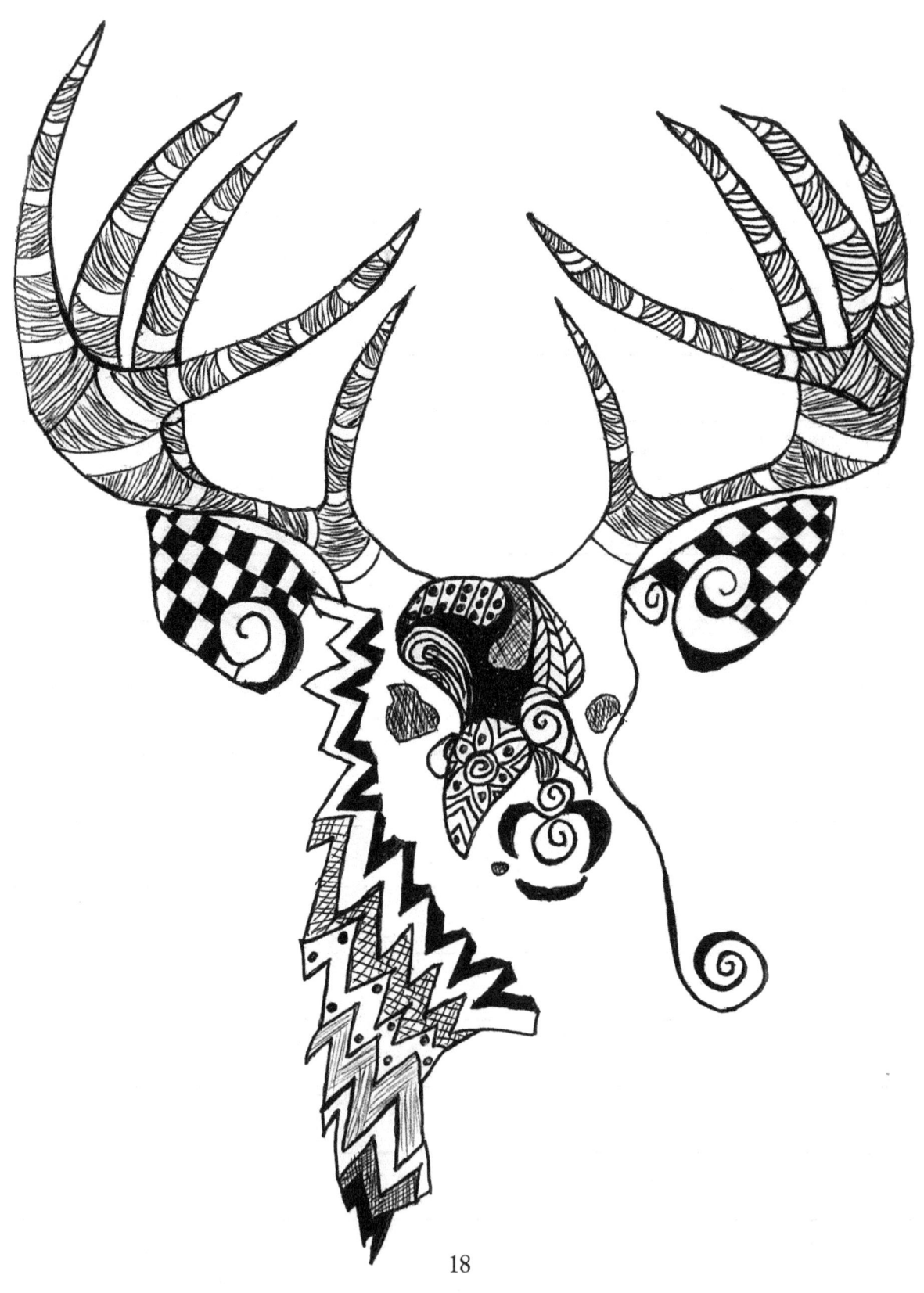

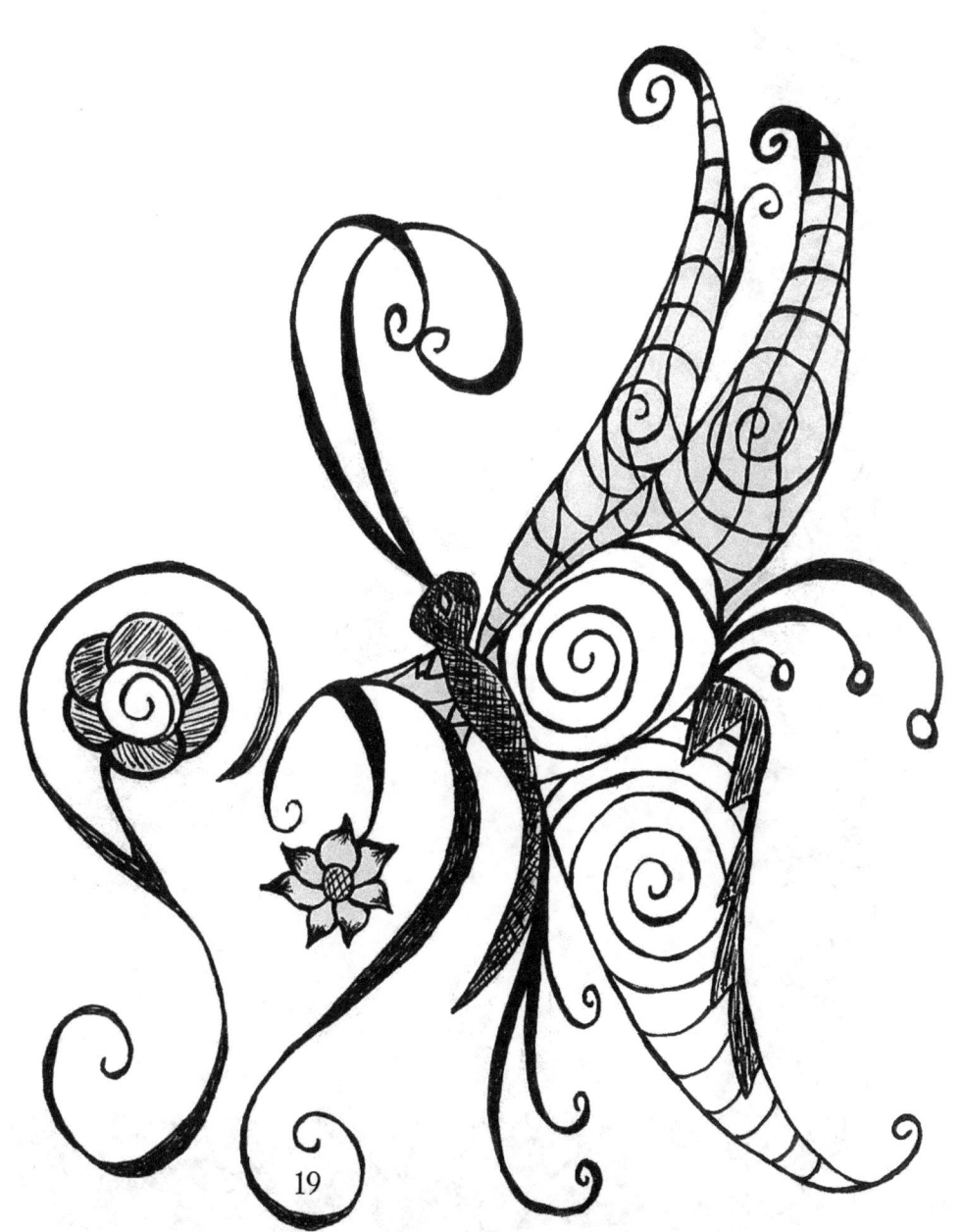

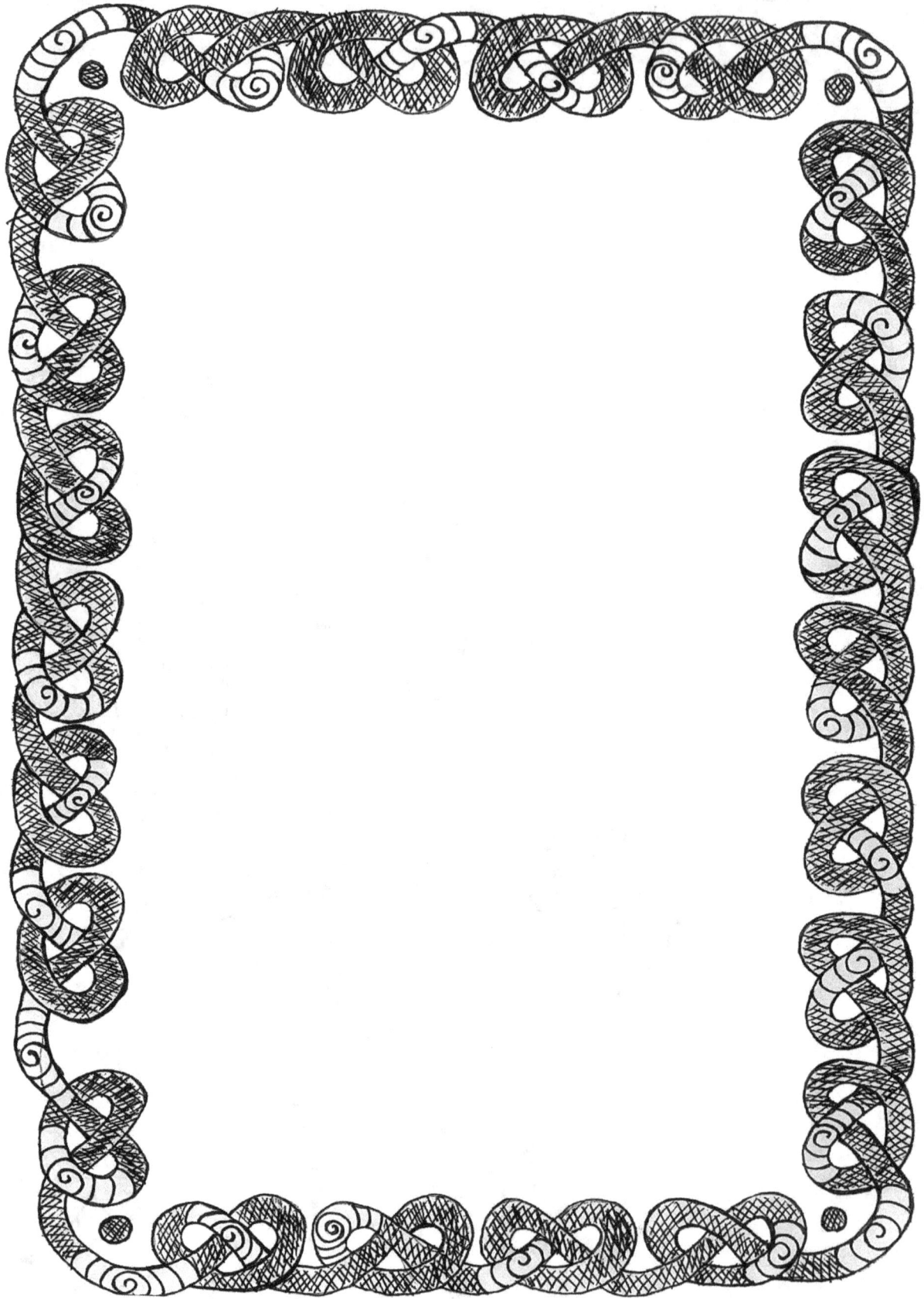

Dum Spiro, Spero-

While I breathe, I hope.

-Cicero

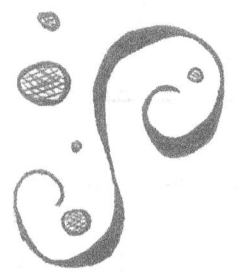
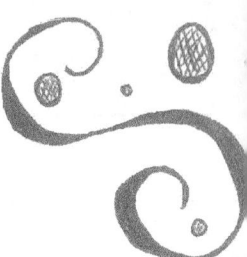

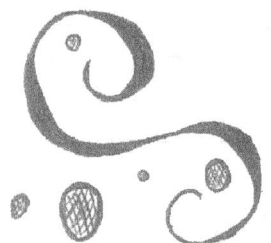
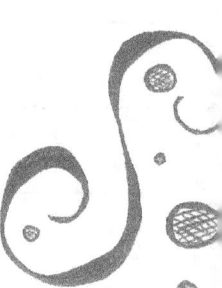

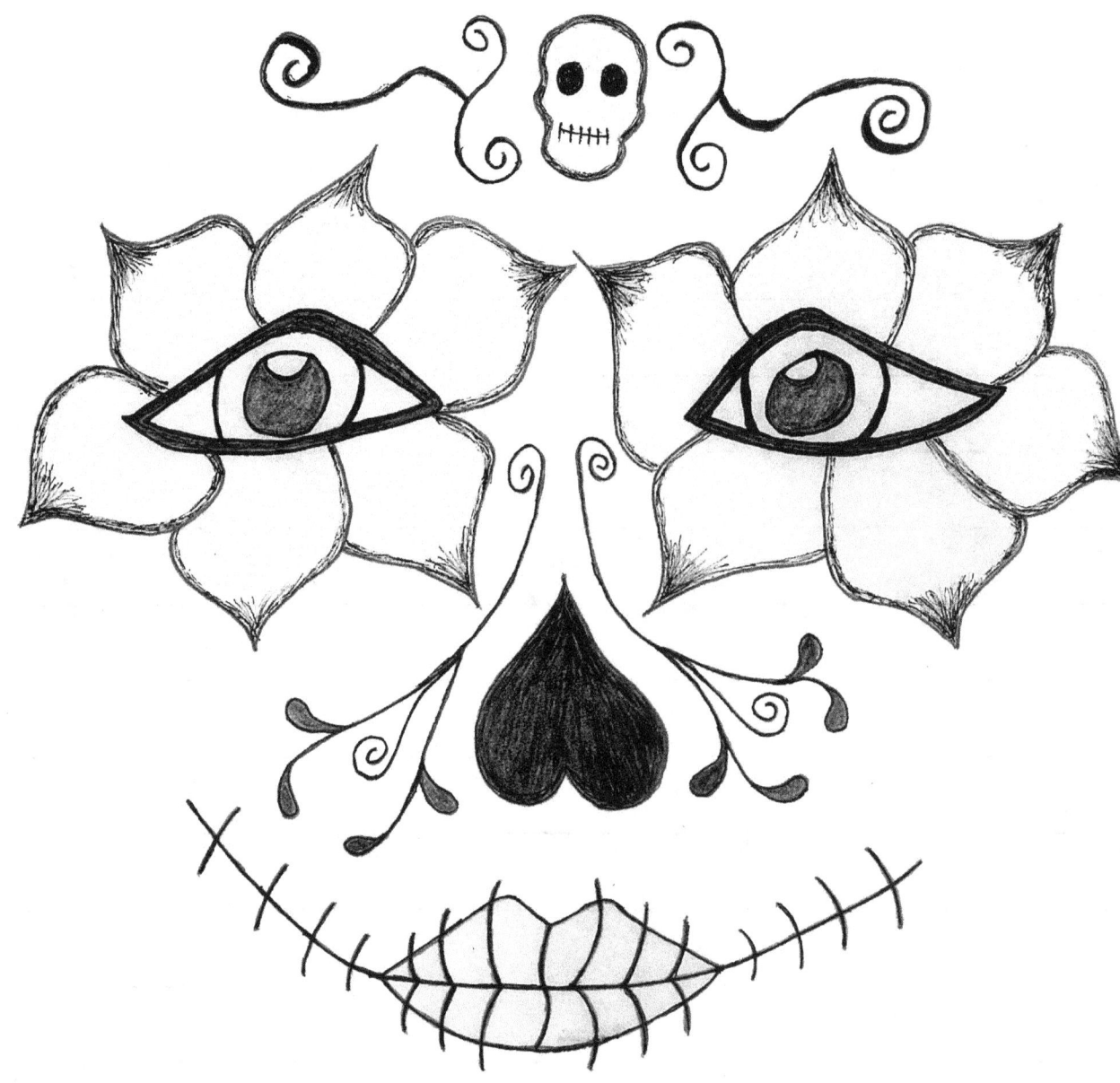

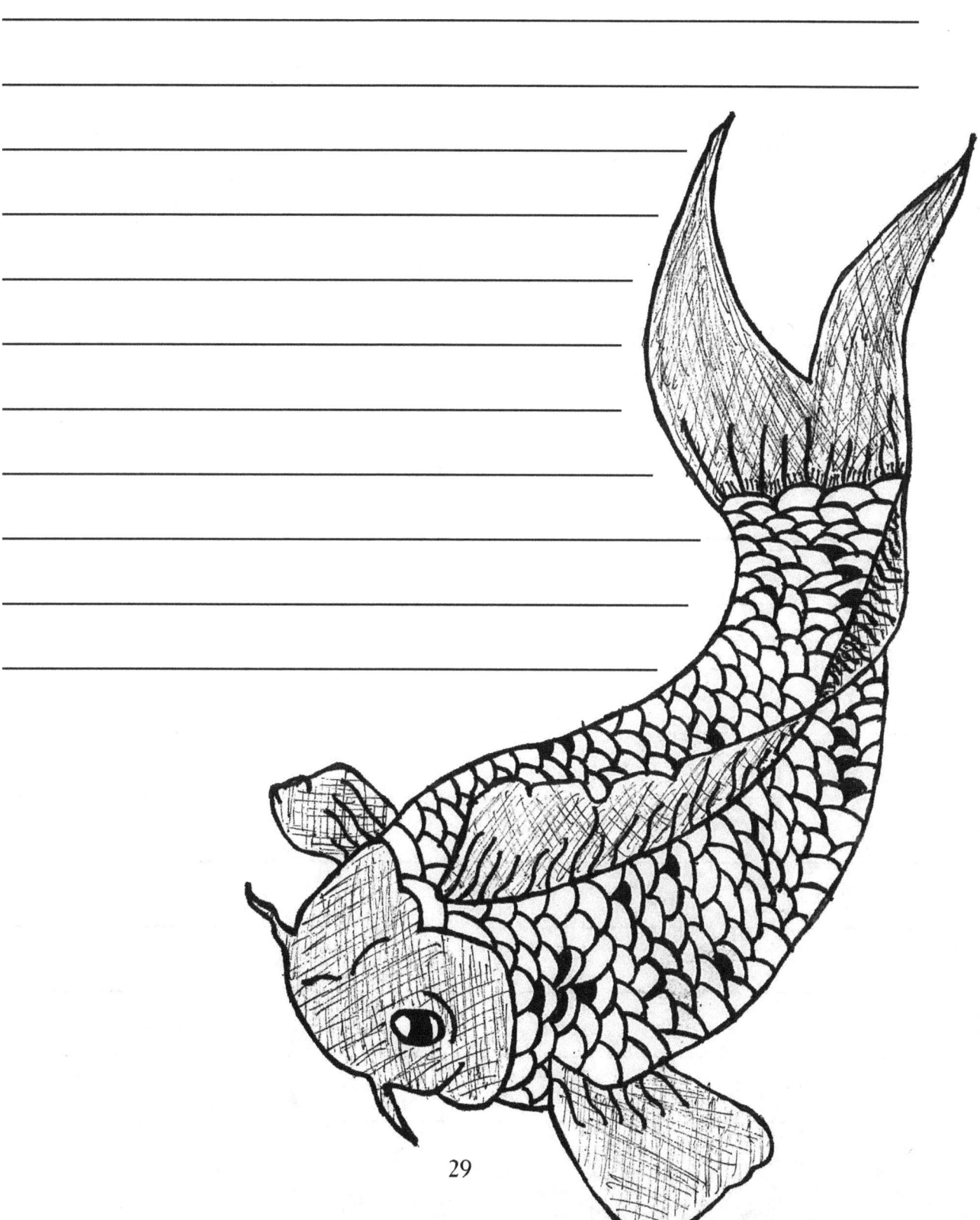

29

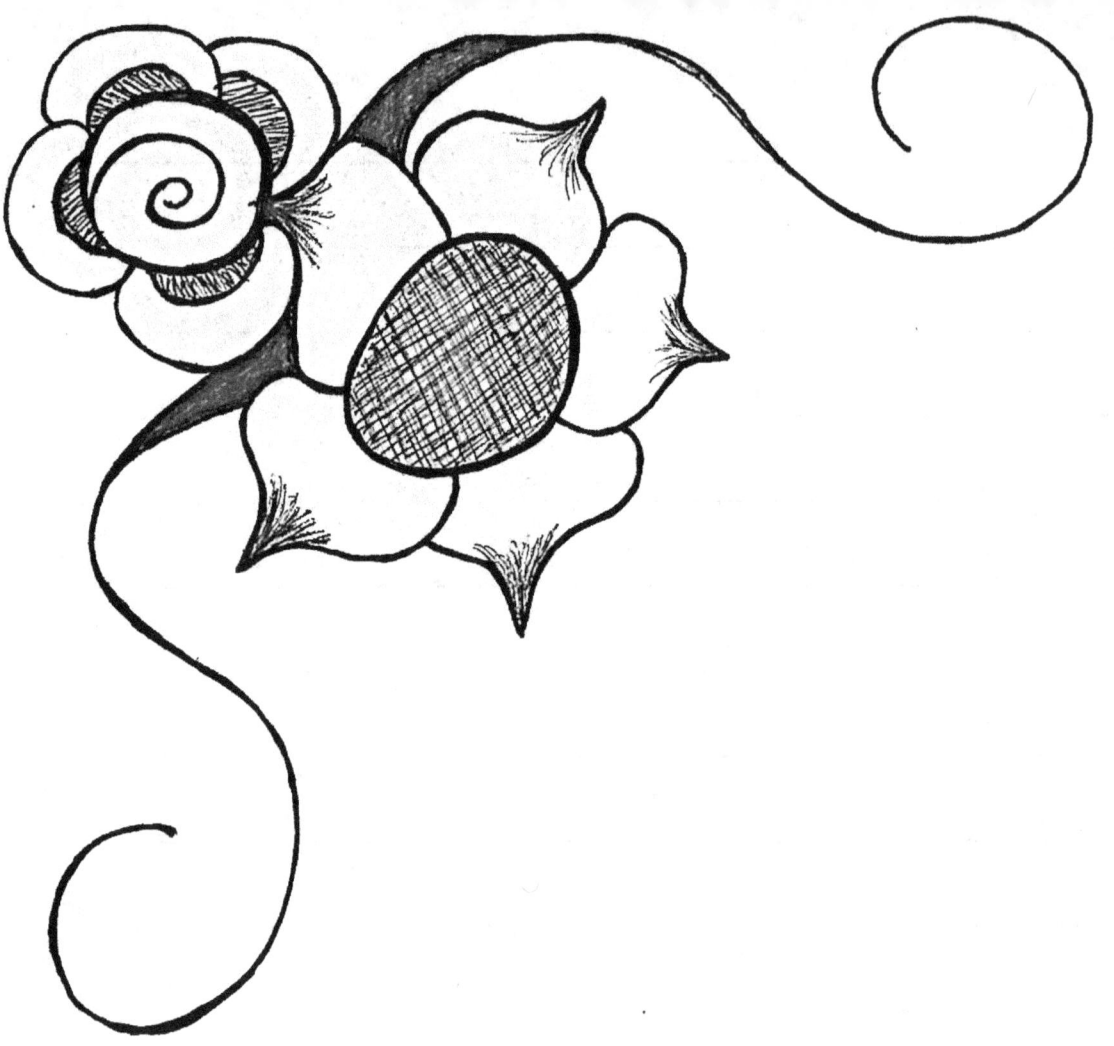

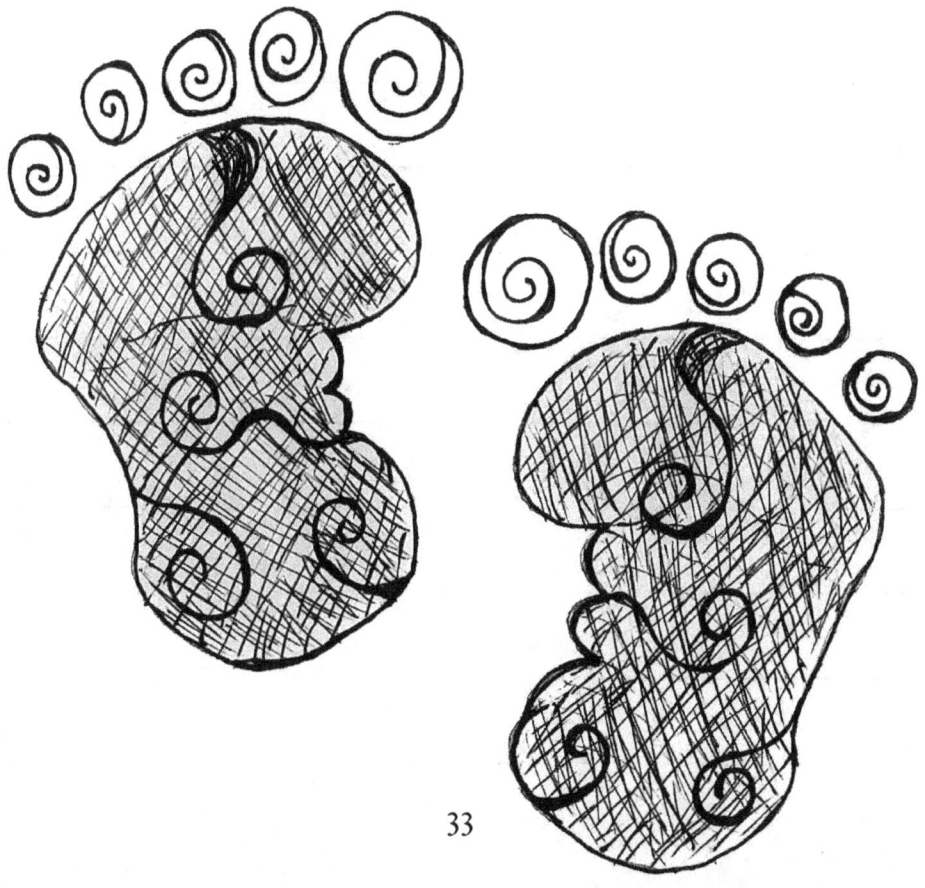

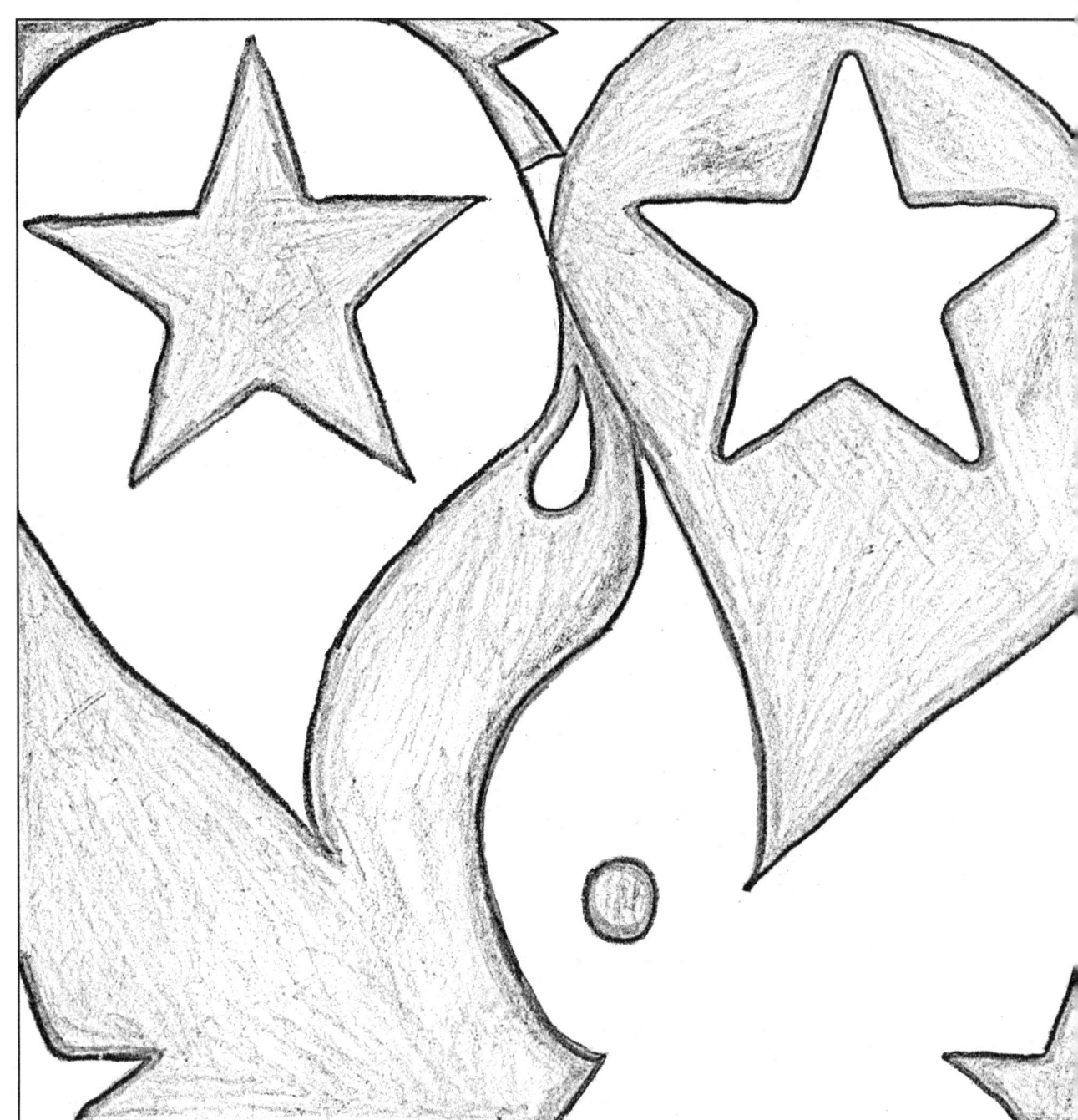

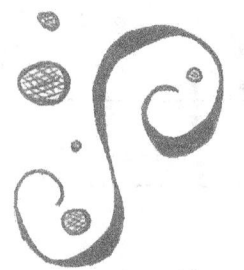
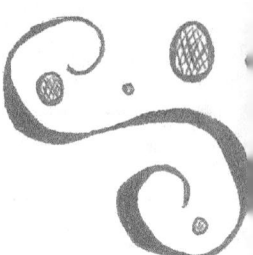

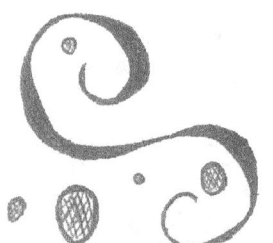
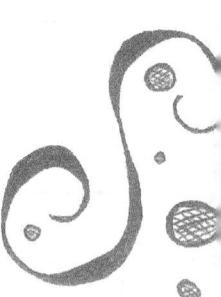

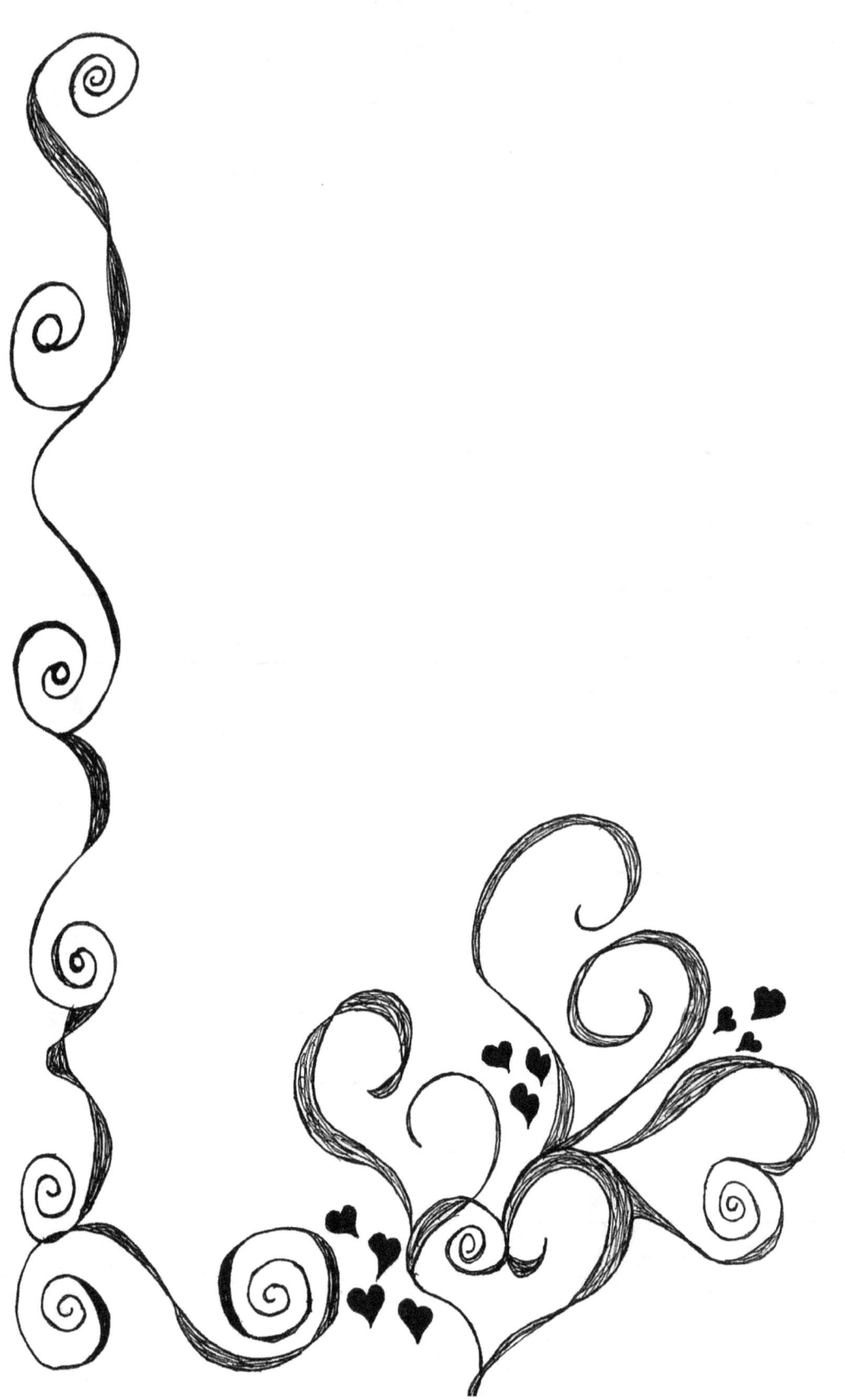

Sapere Aude~
Dare to be wise.

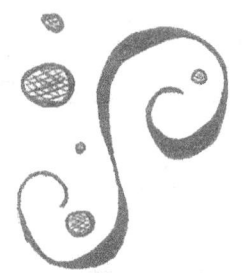
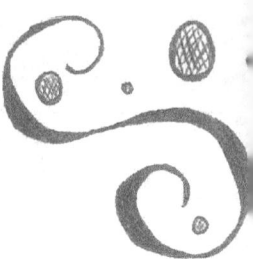

46

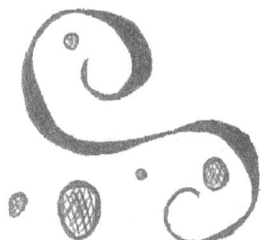
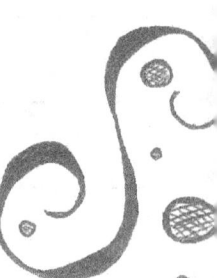

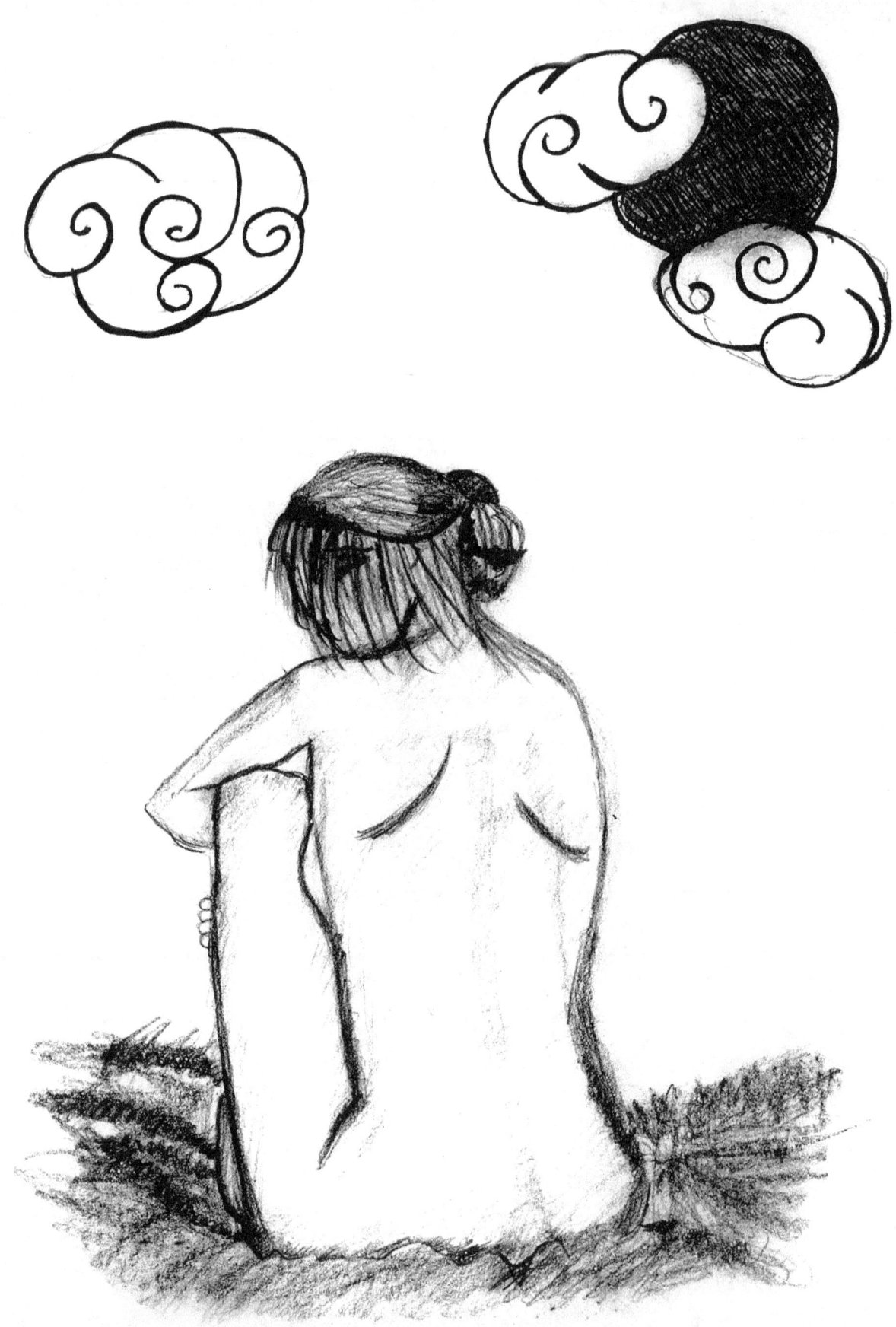

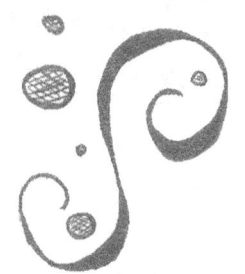
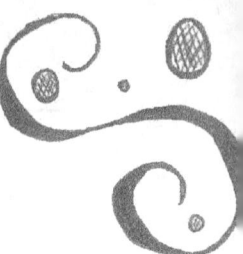

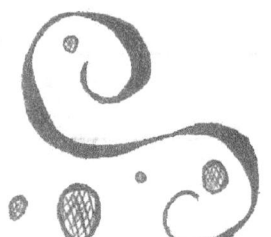
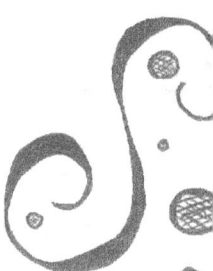

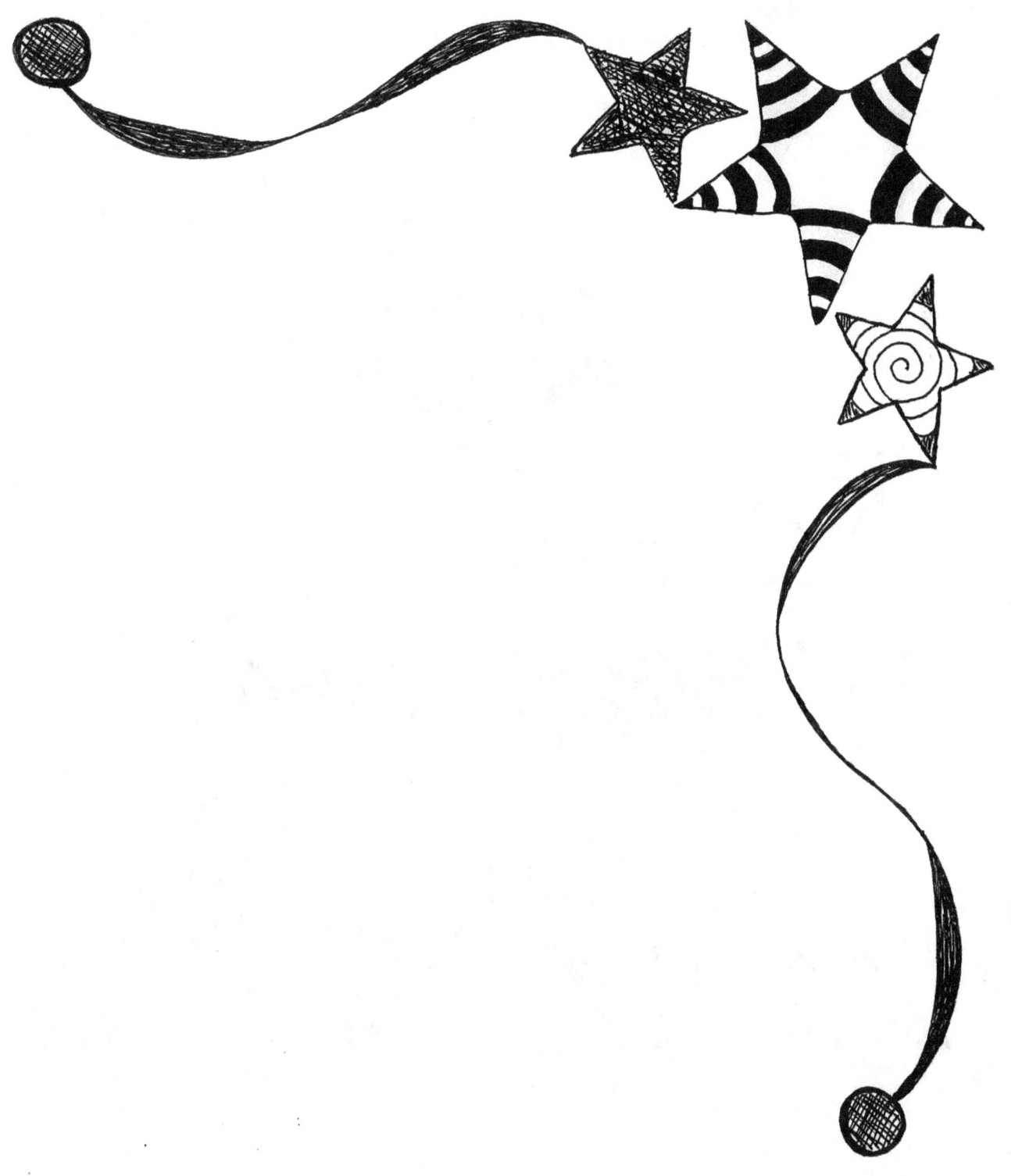

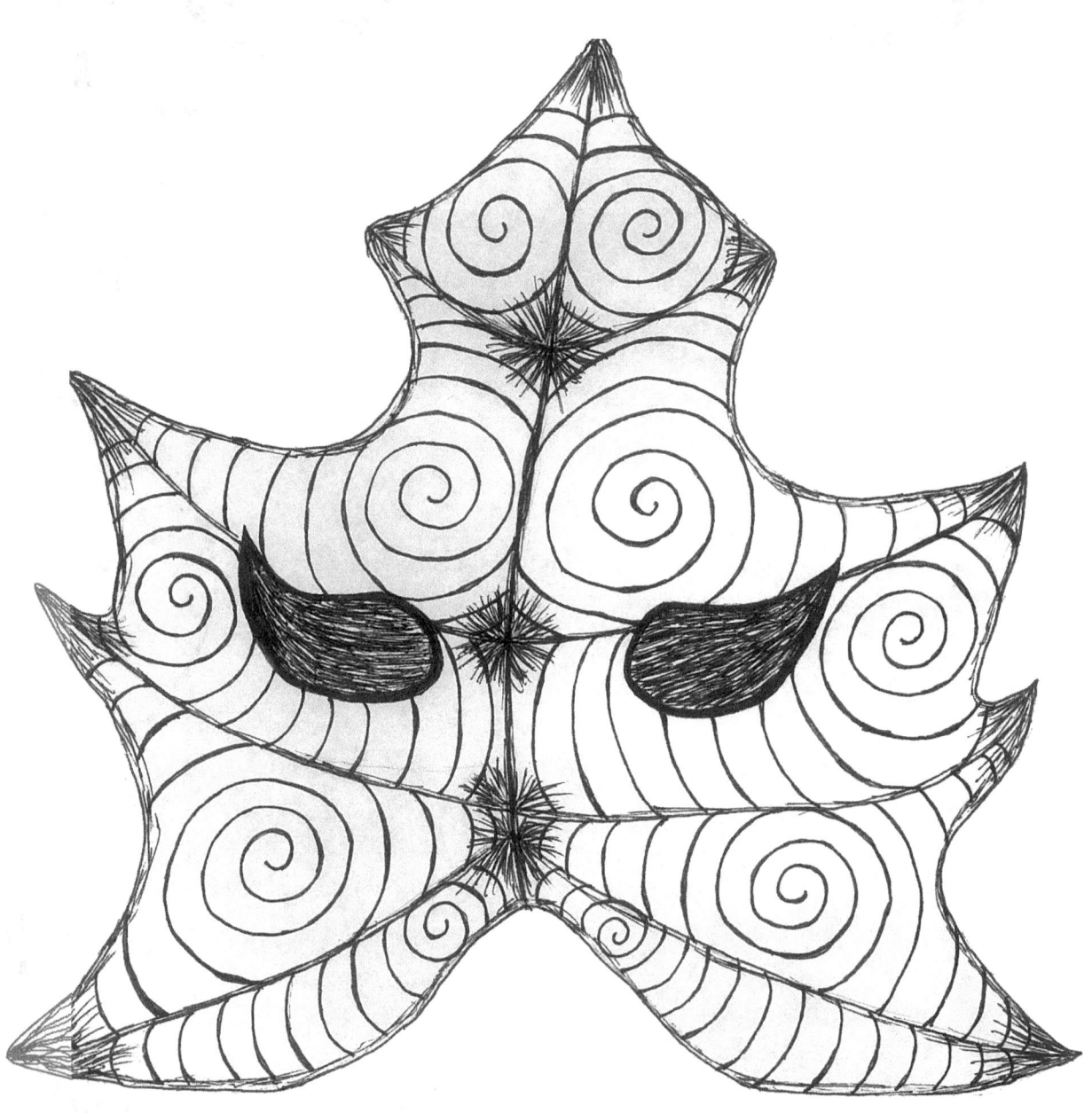

54

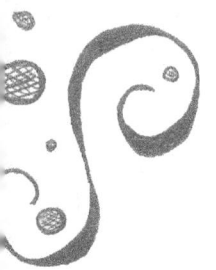
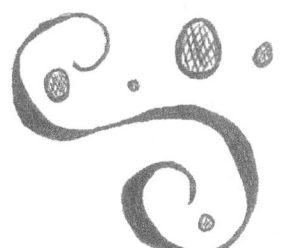

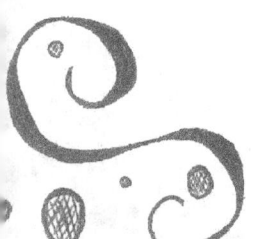
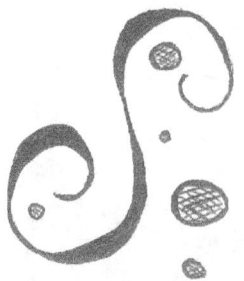

Semper Liber~
Always Free

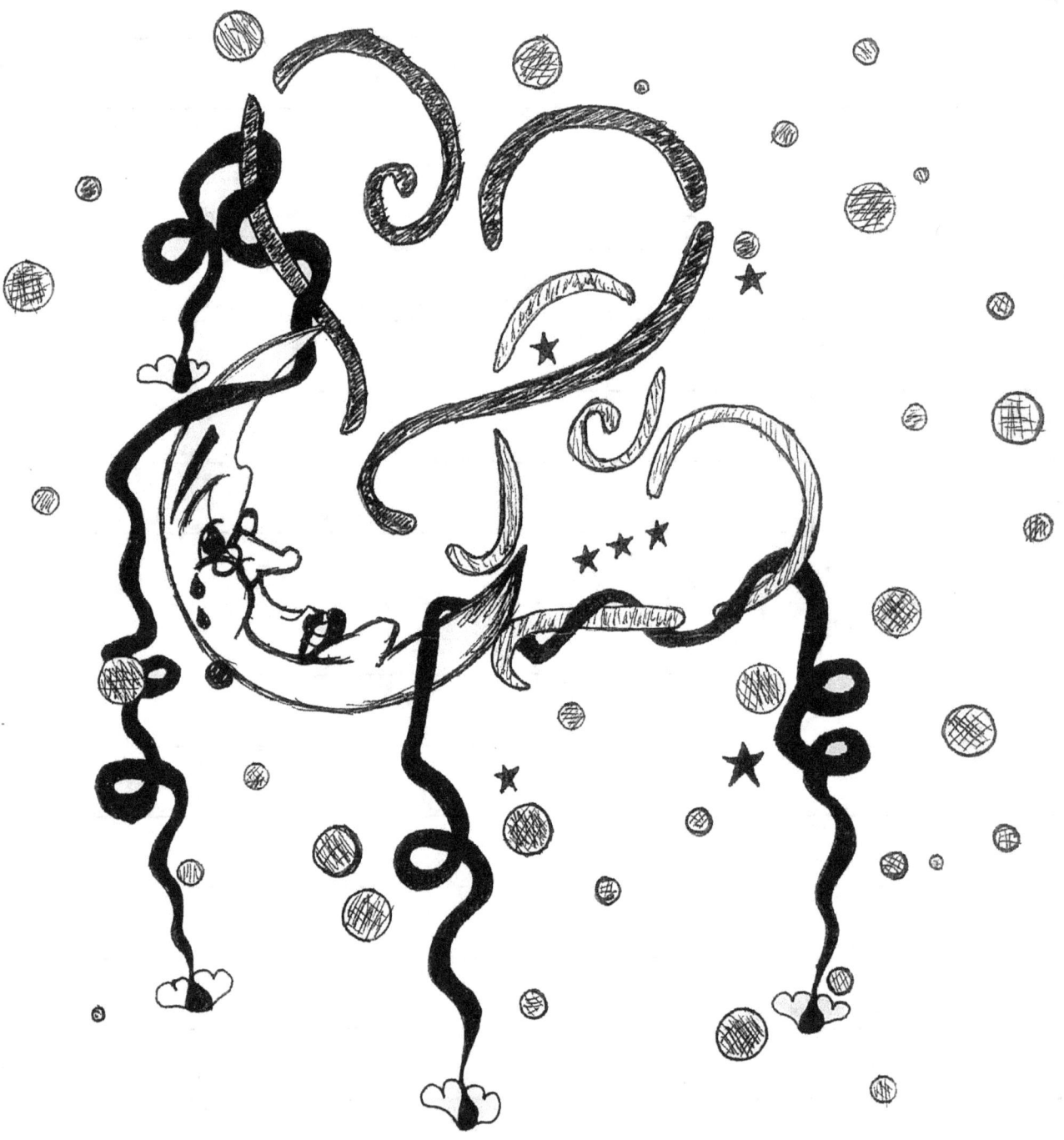

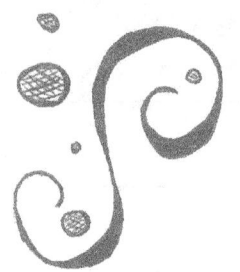
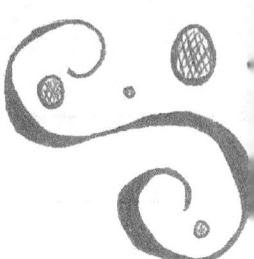

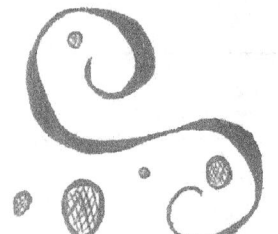
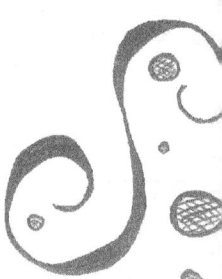

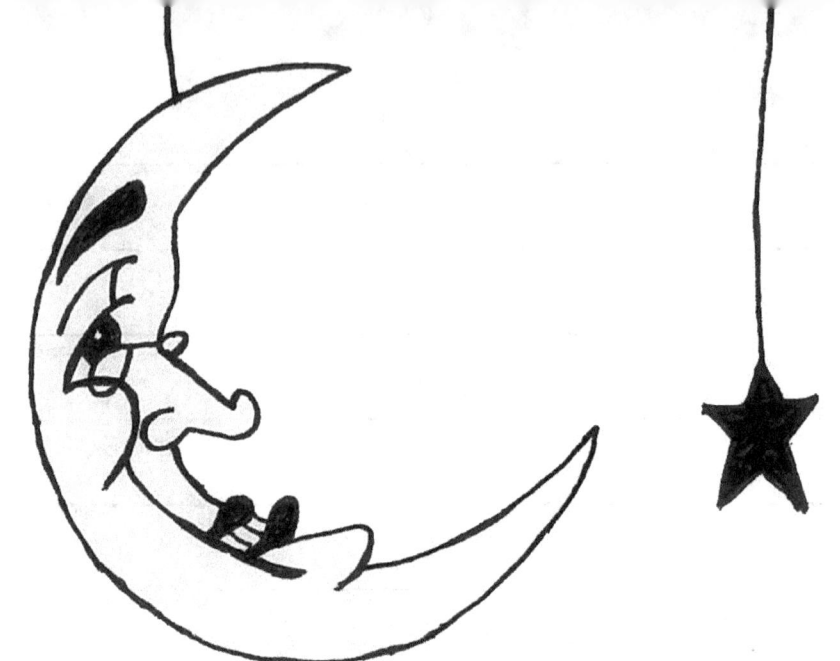

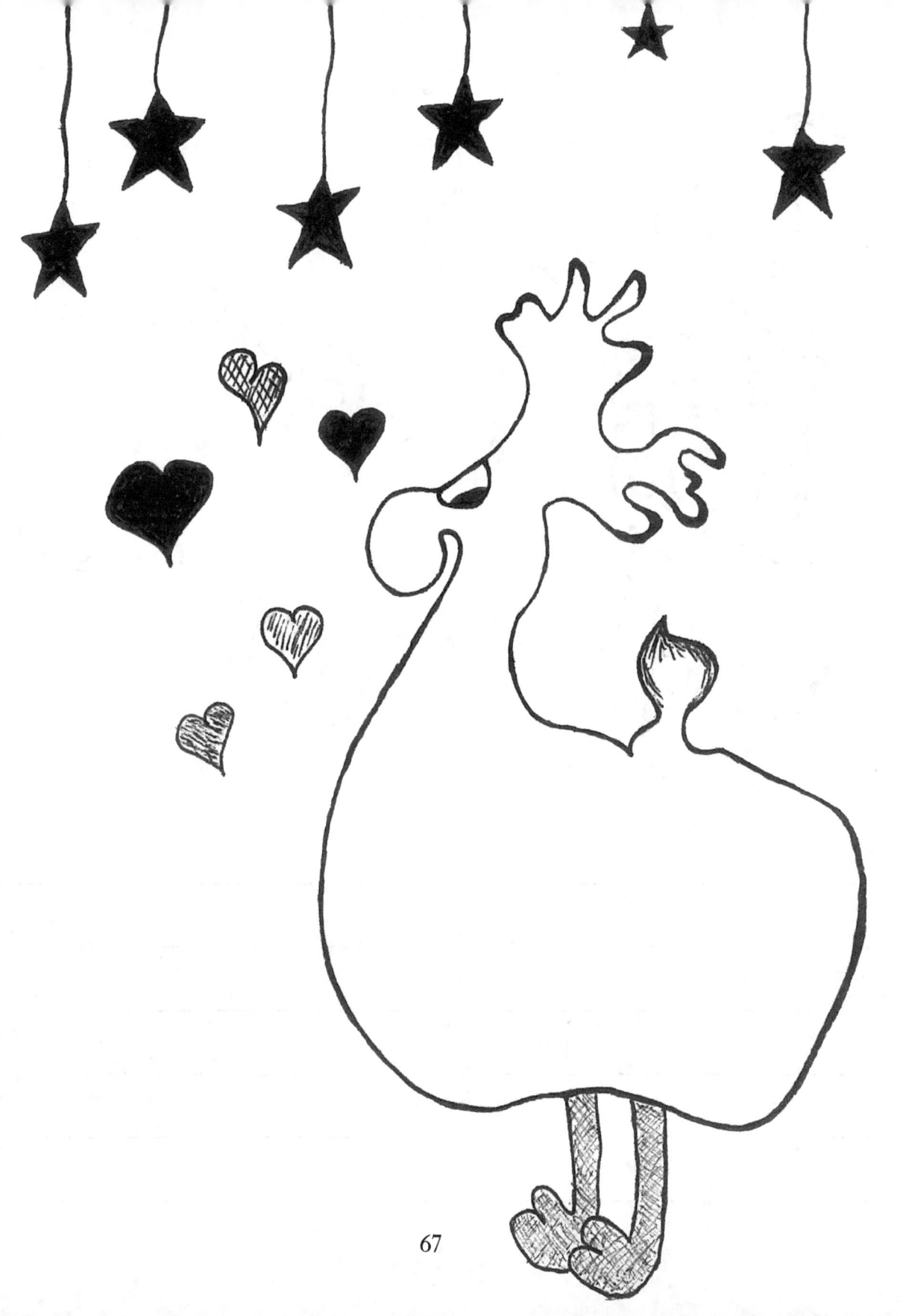

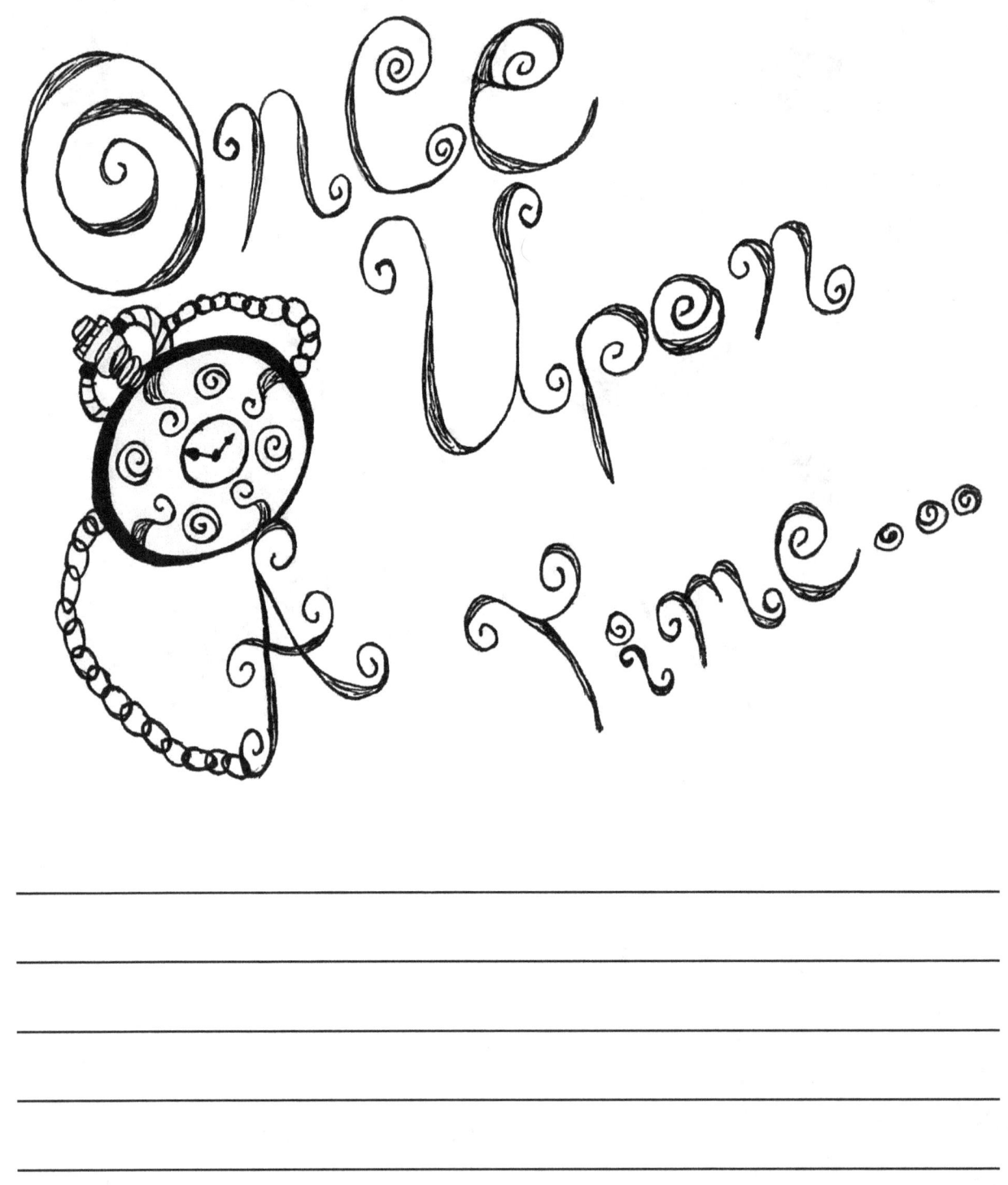

Veni vidi Vinci~

I came,

I saw,

I conquered.

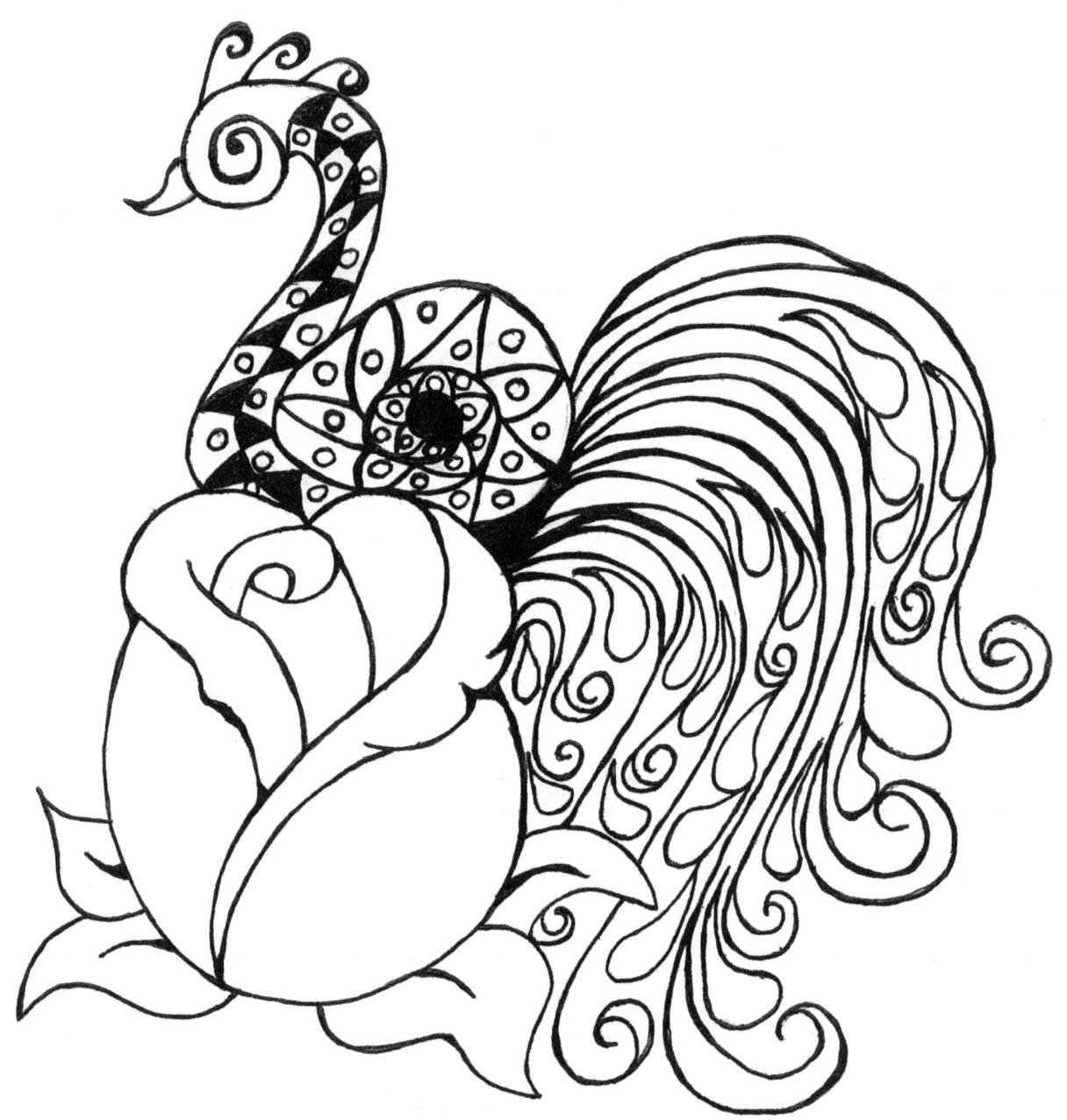

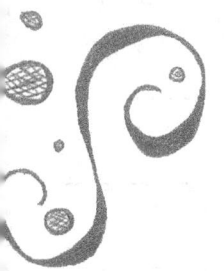
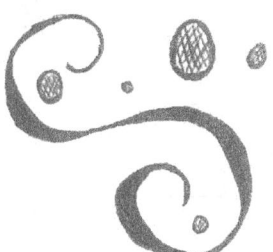
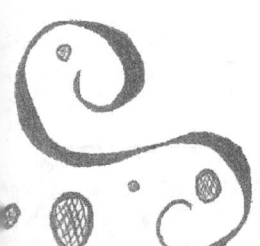
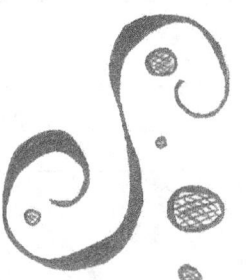

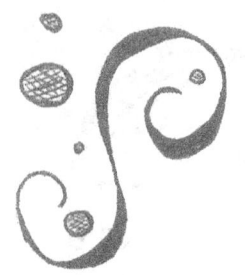
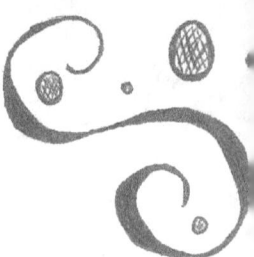

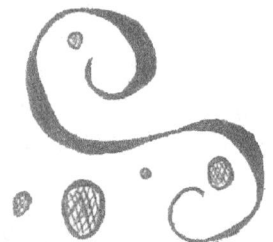
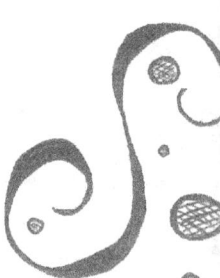

Carpe Diem~

Seize the day.

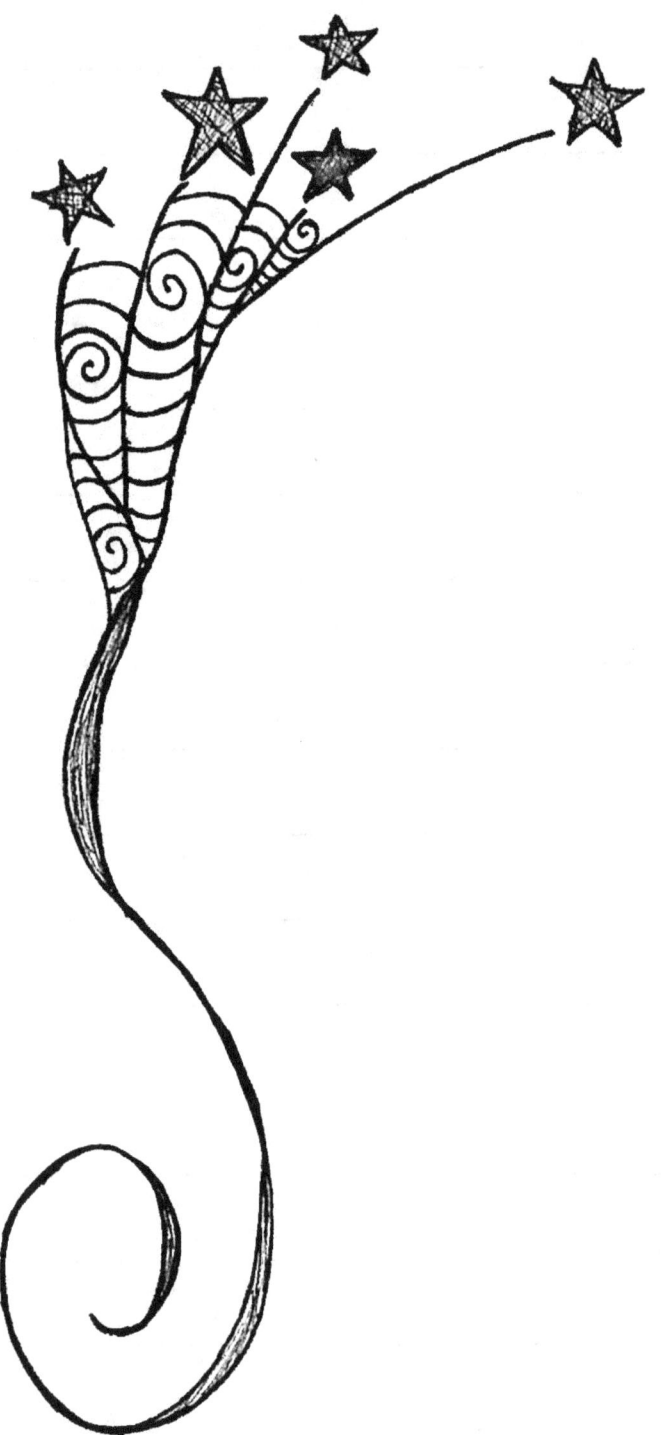

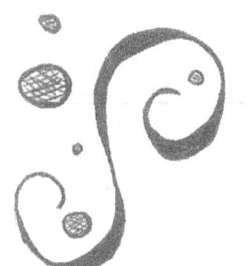
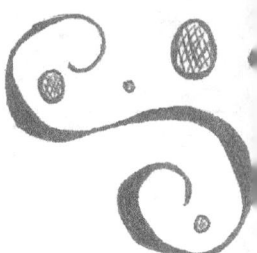

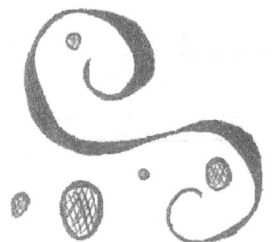
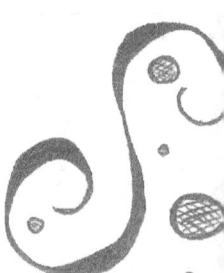

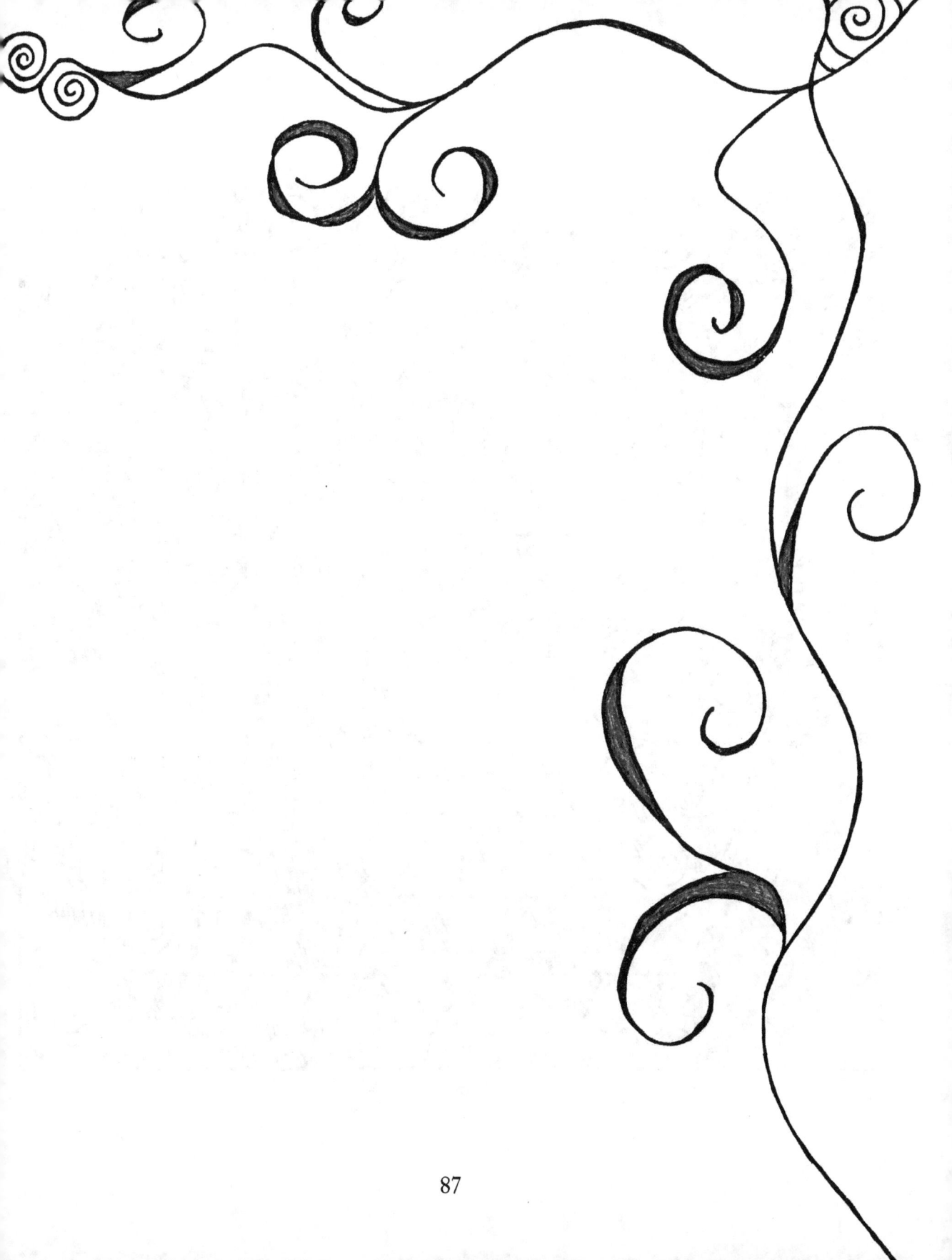

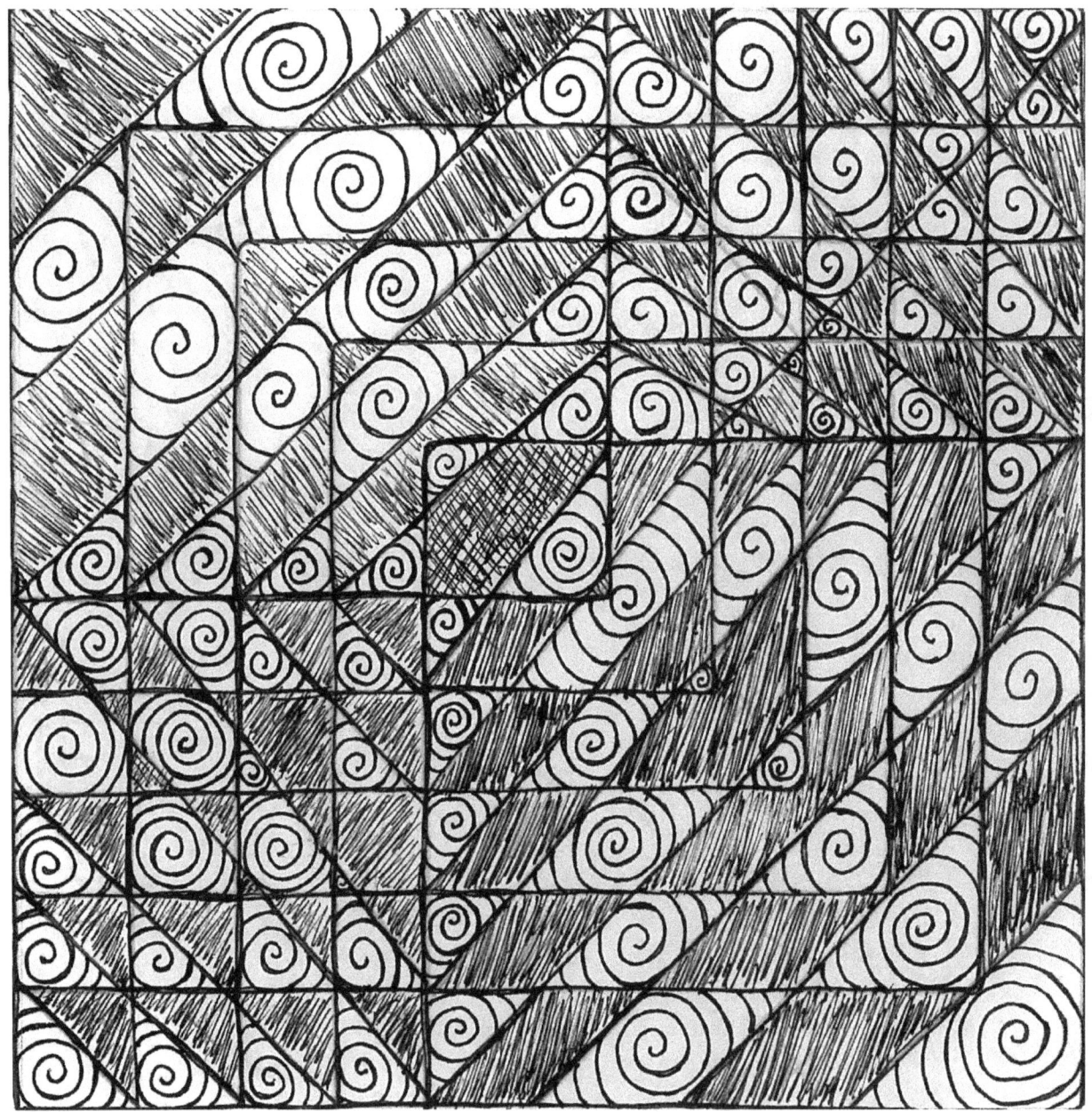

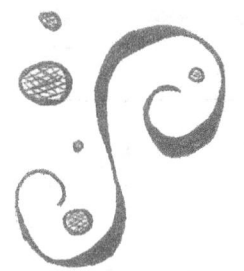
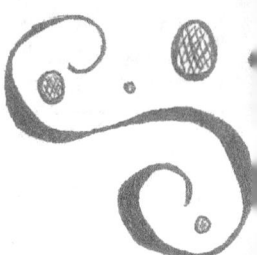

90

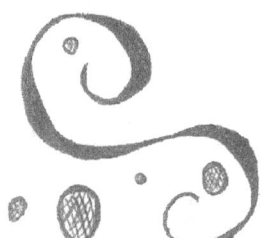
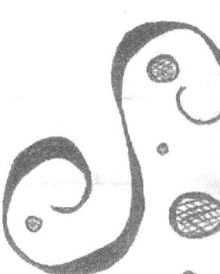

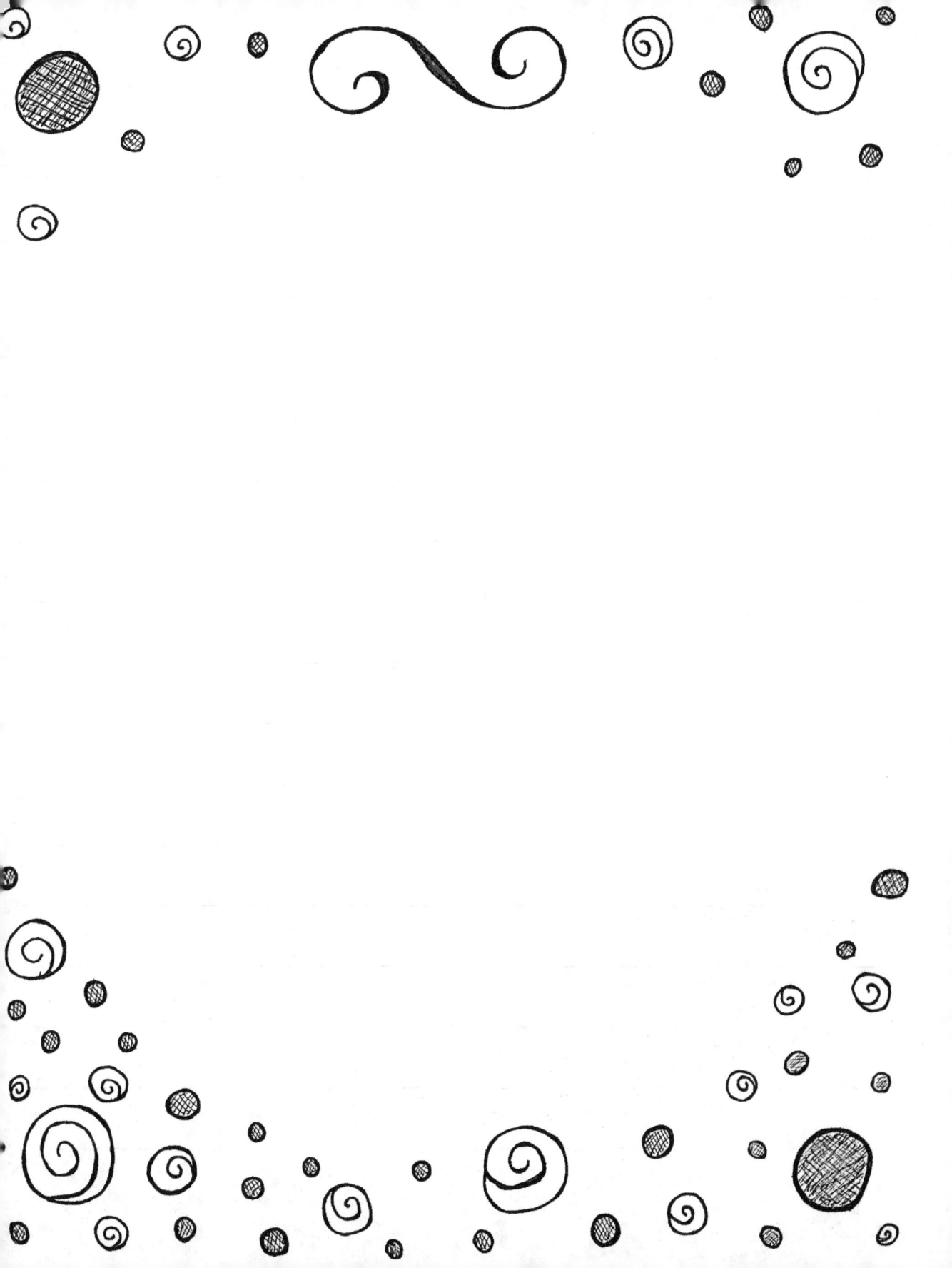

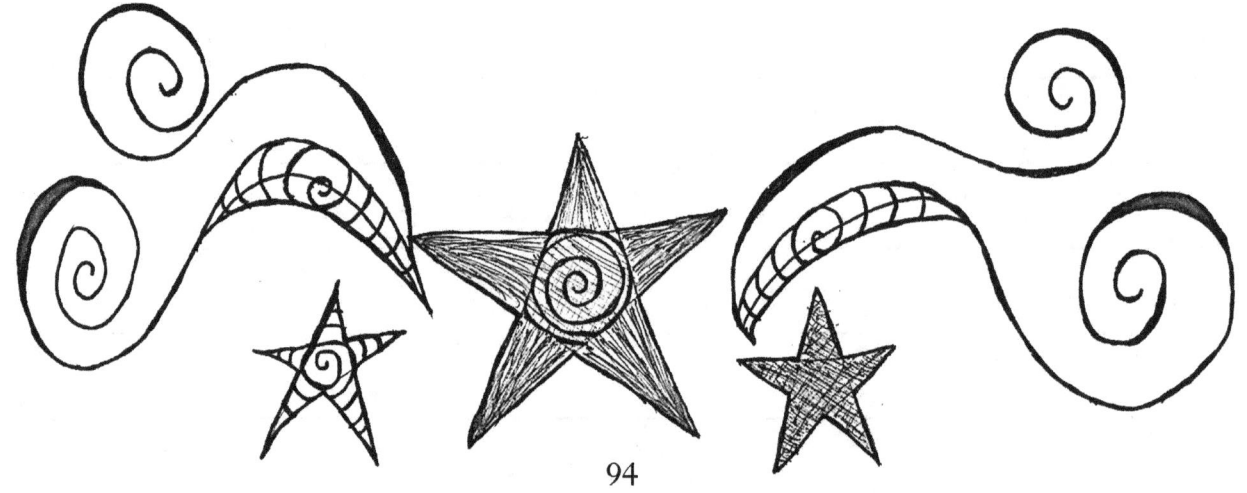

94

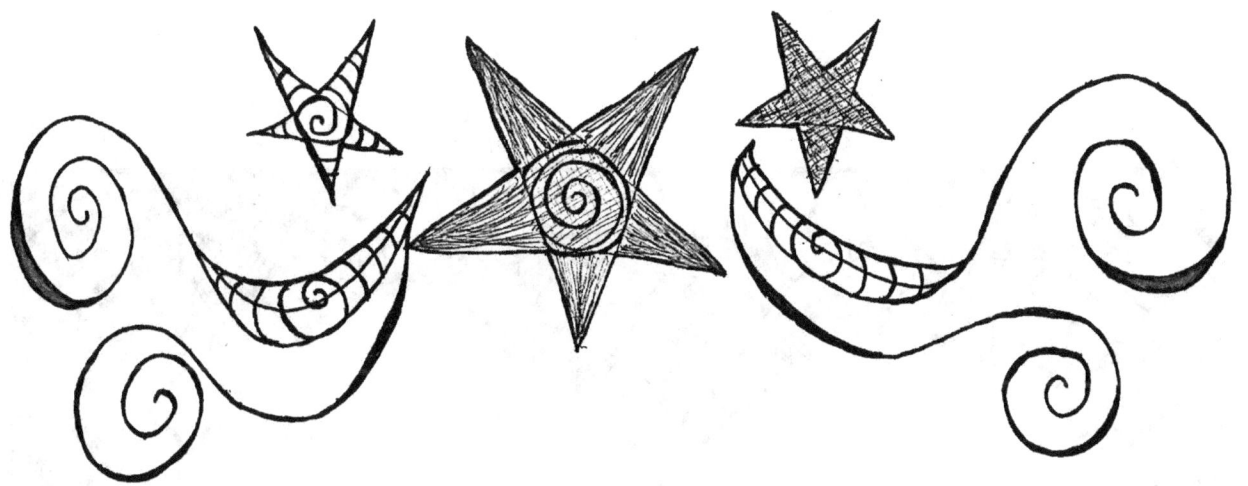

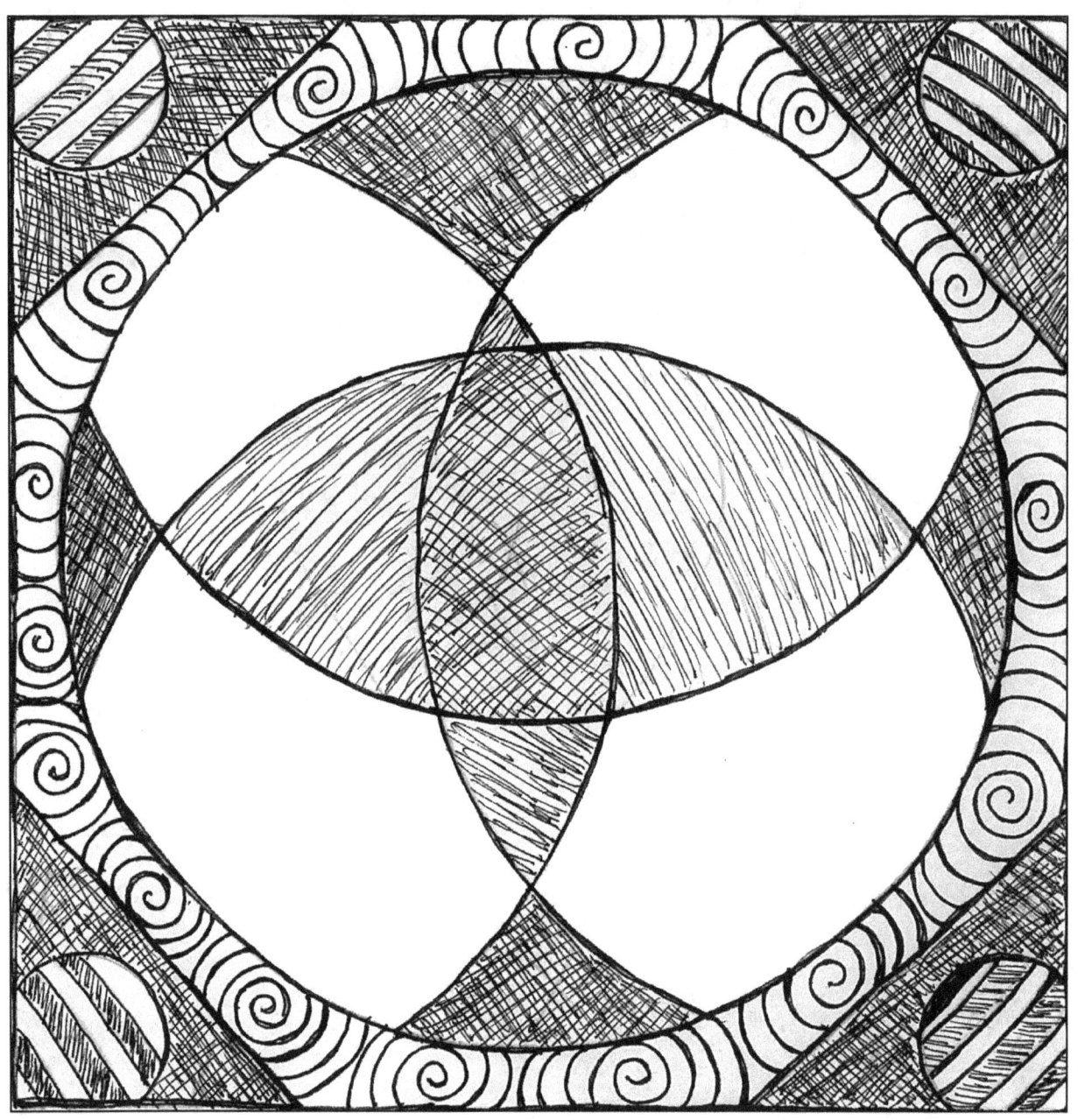

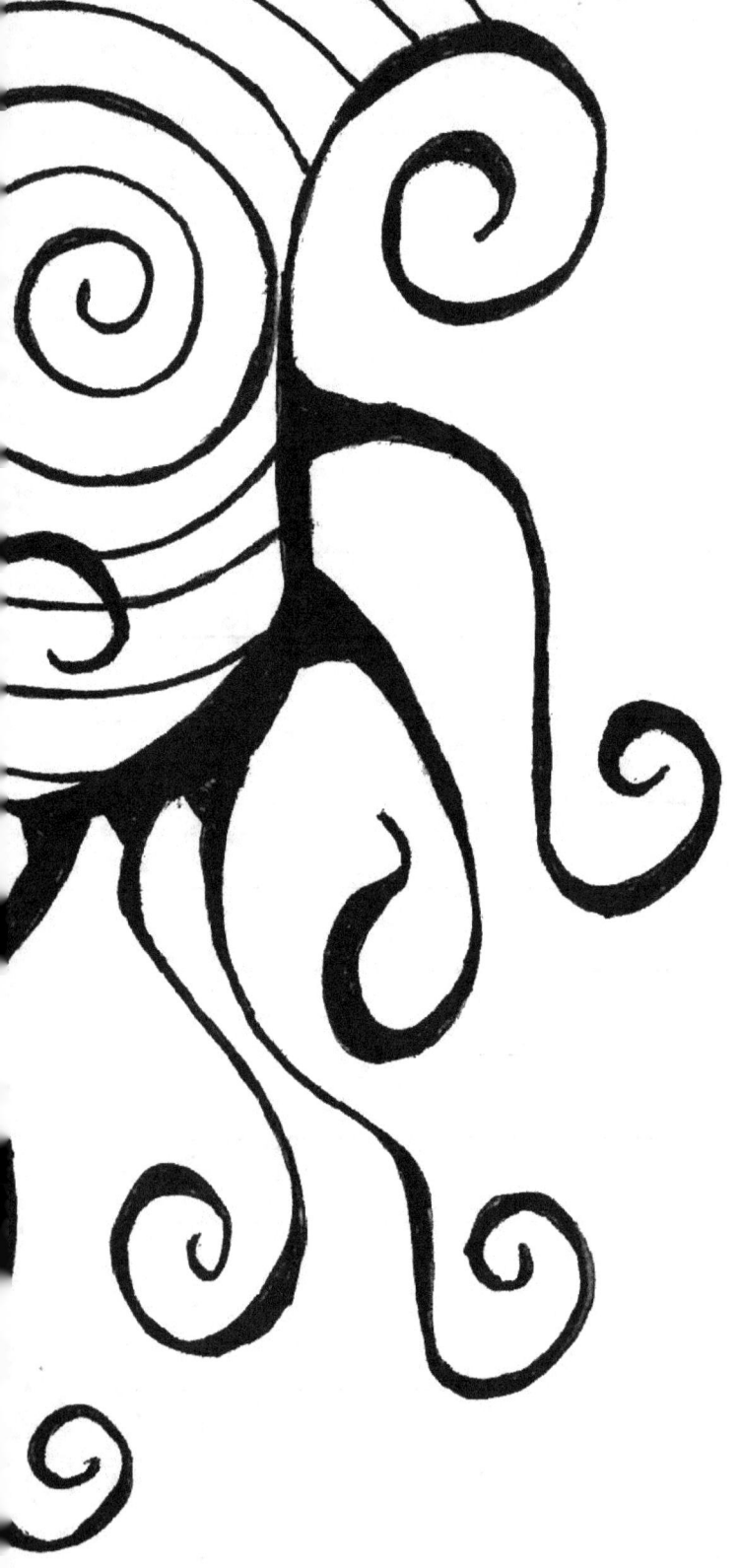

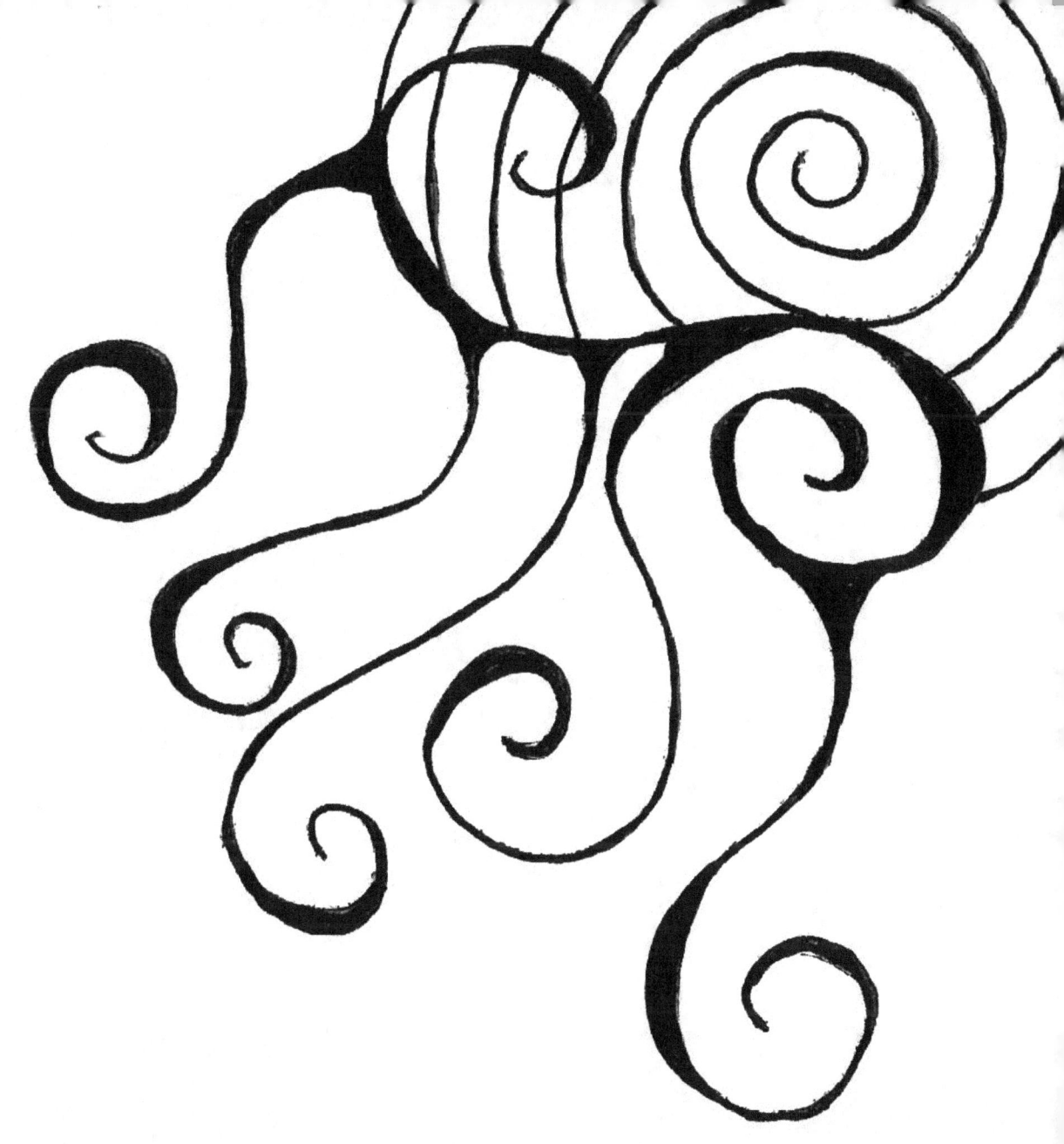

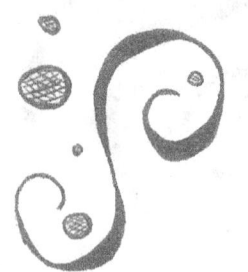
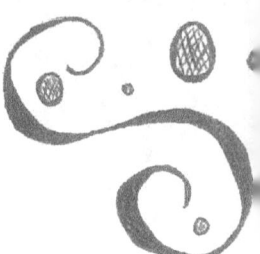

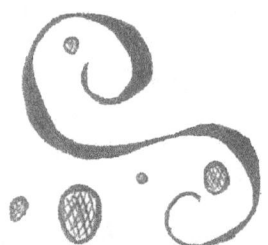
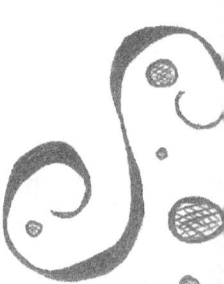

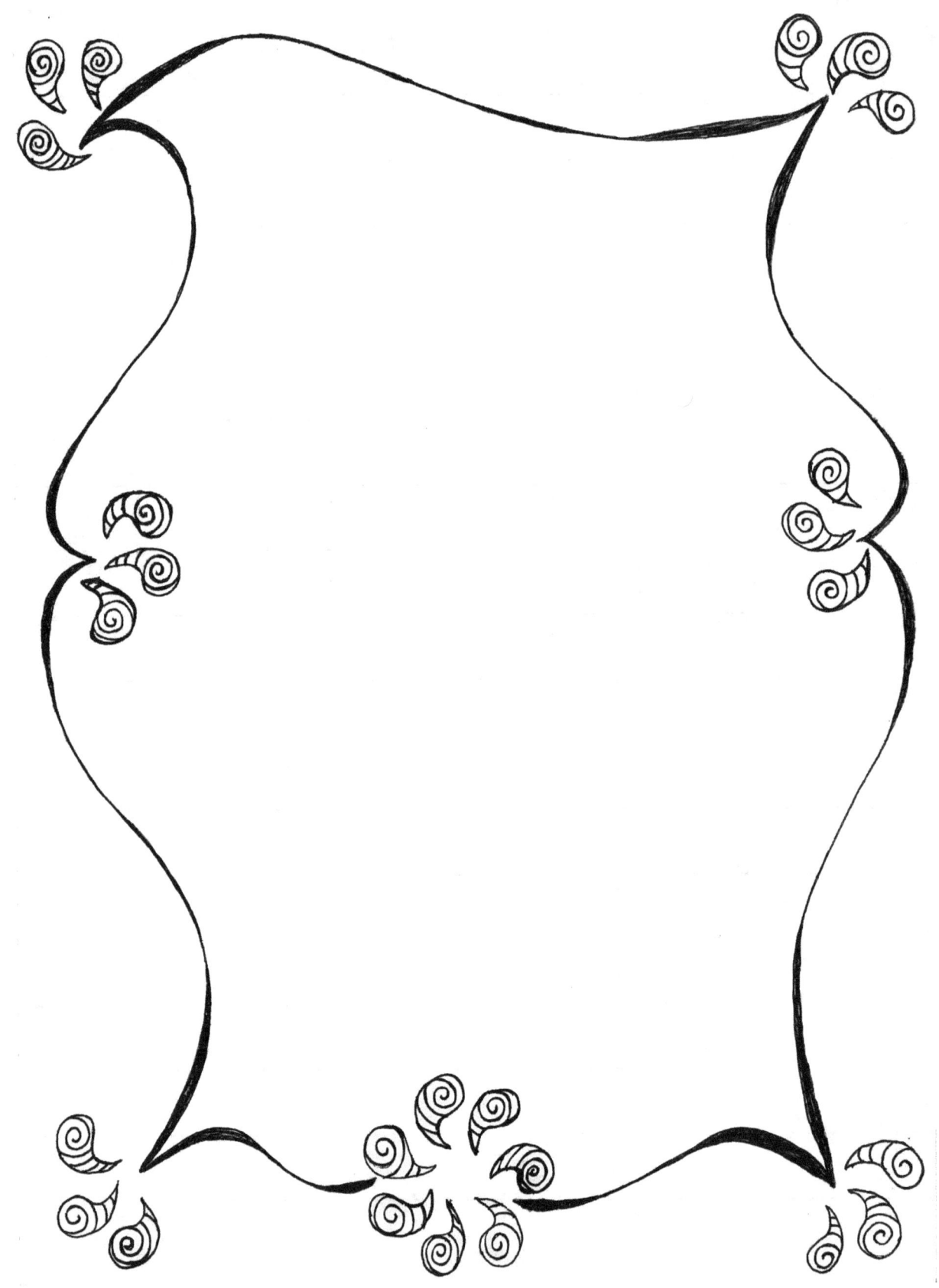

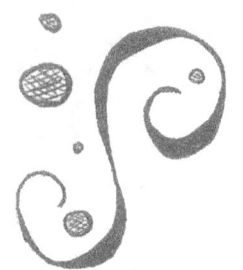
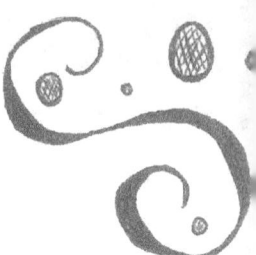

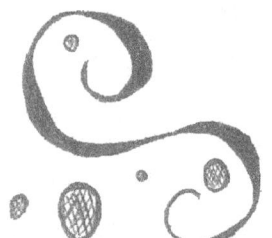
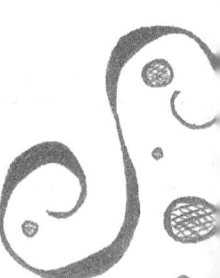

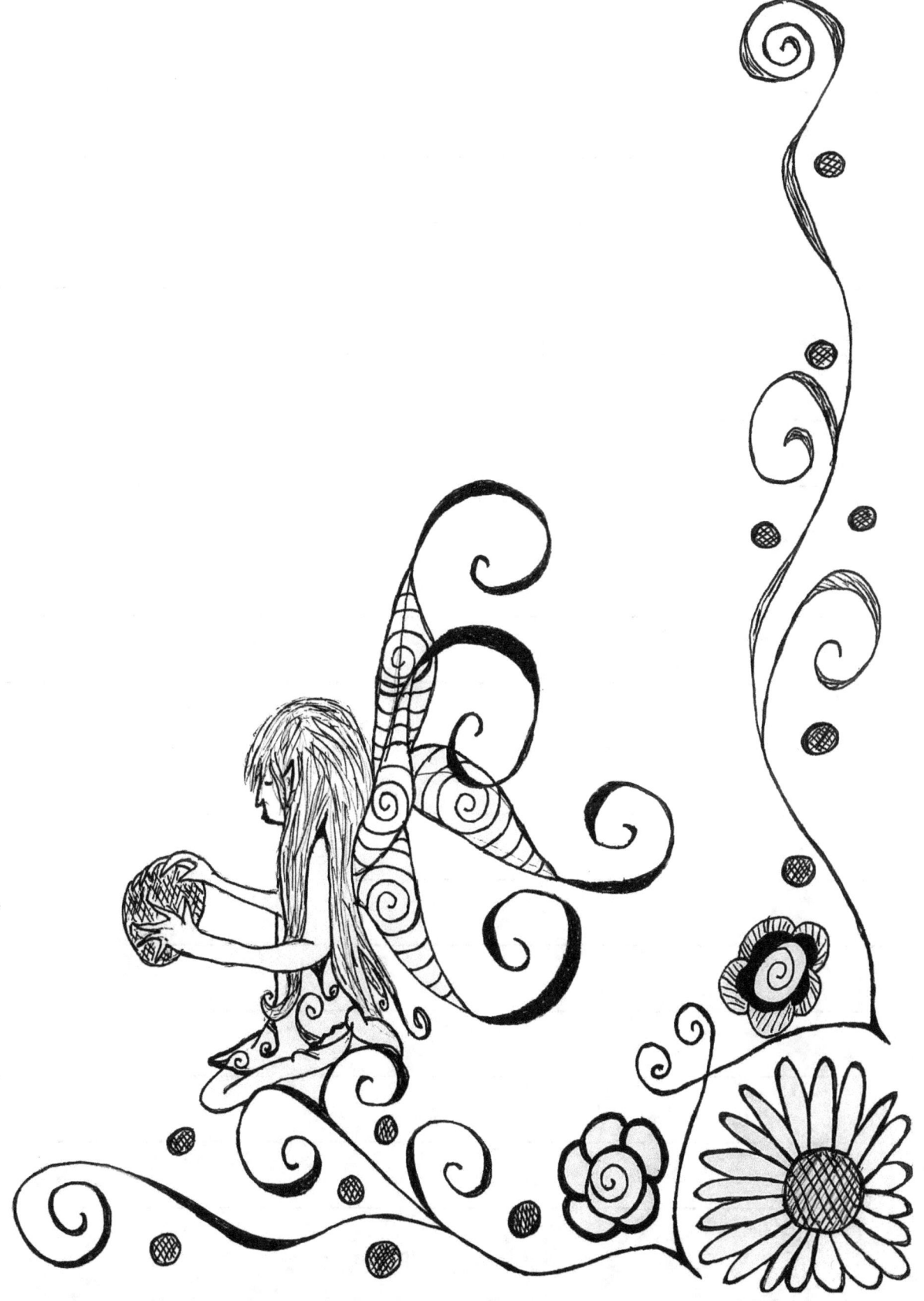

What are men compared to rocks and mountains.

-Jane Austen

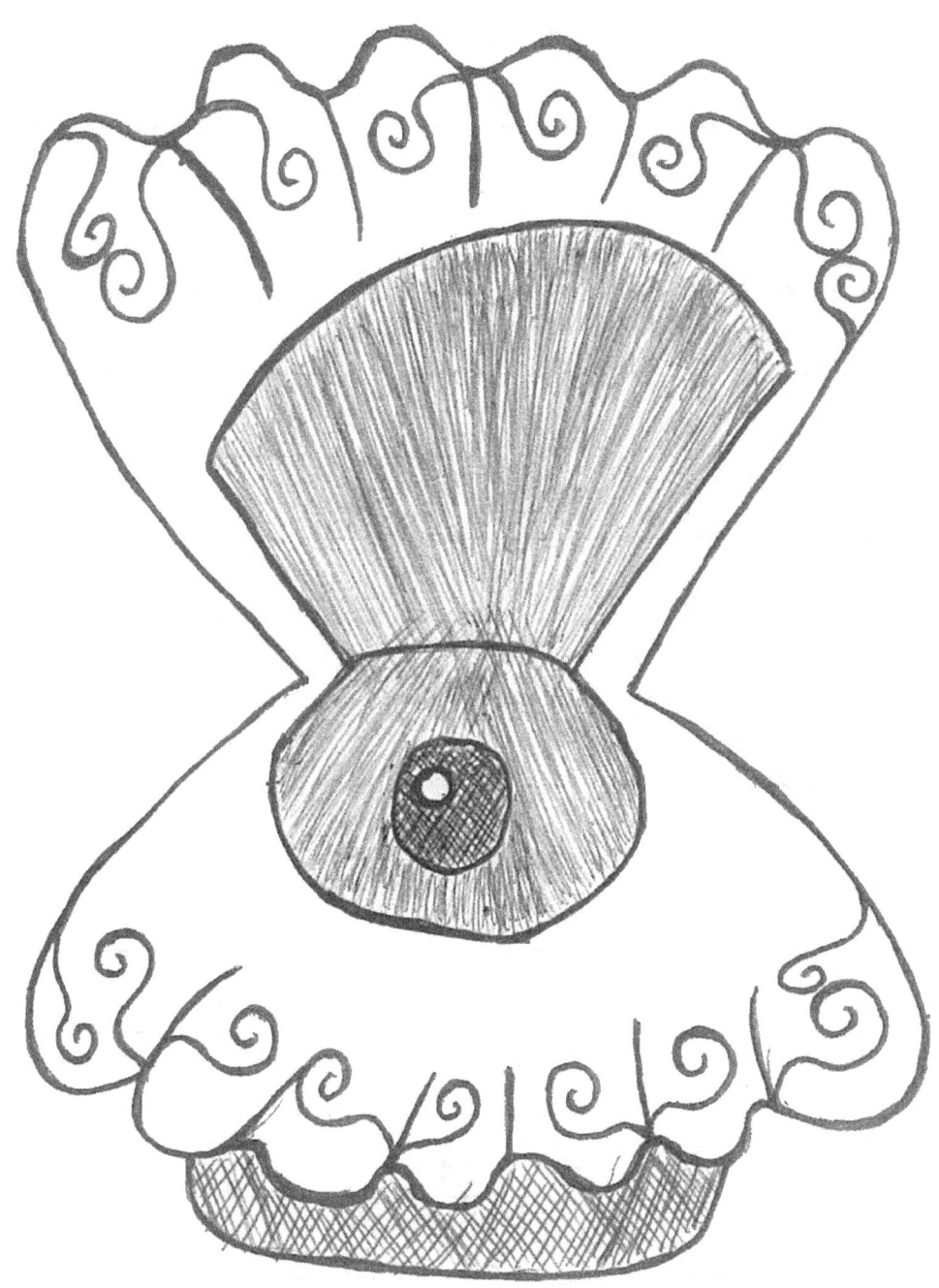

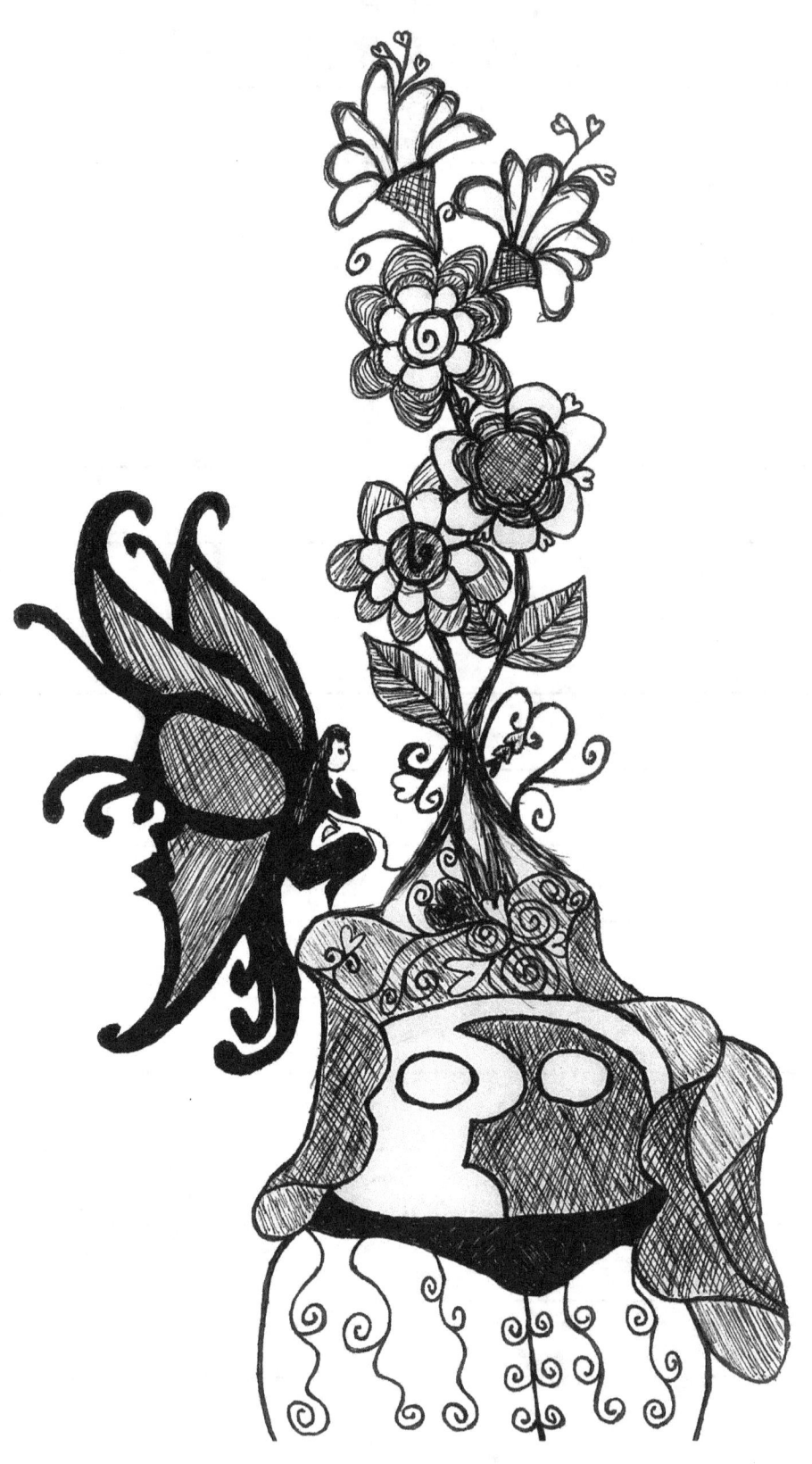

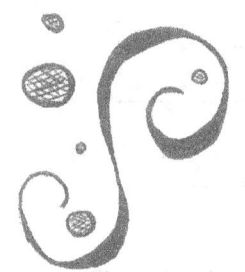
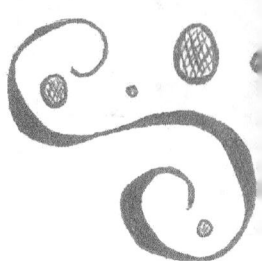

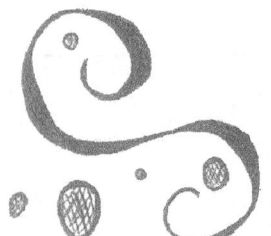
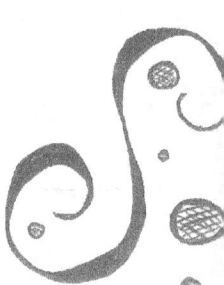

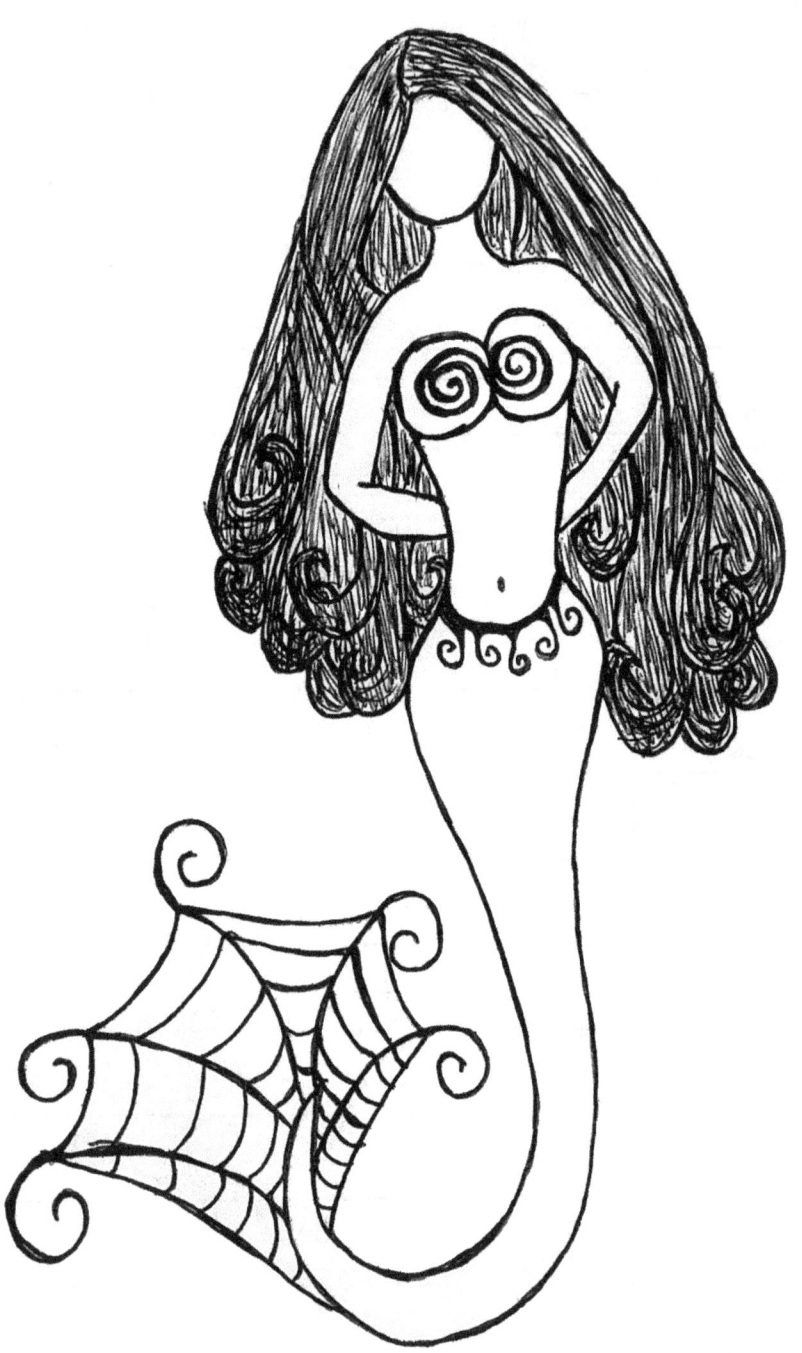

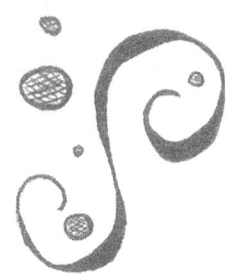
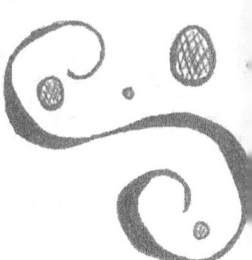

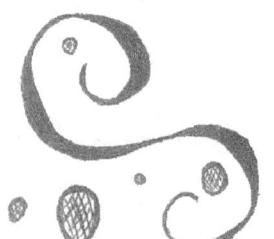
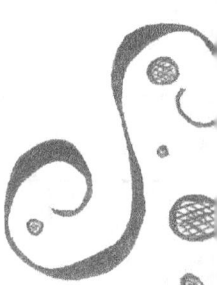

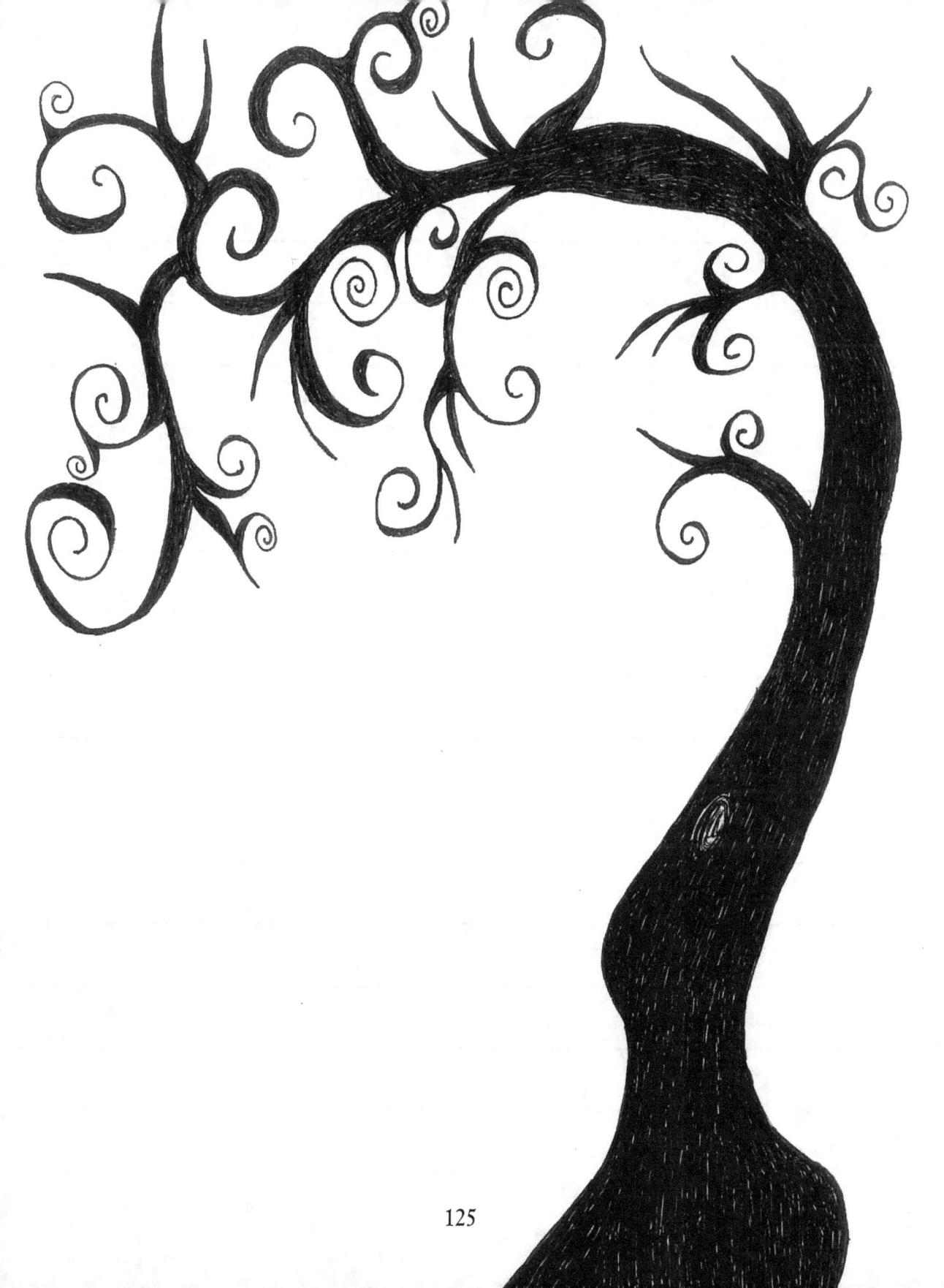

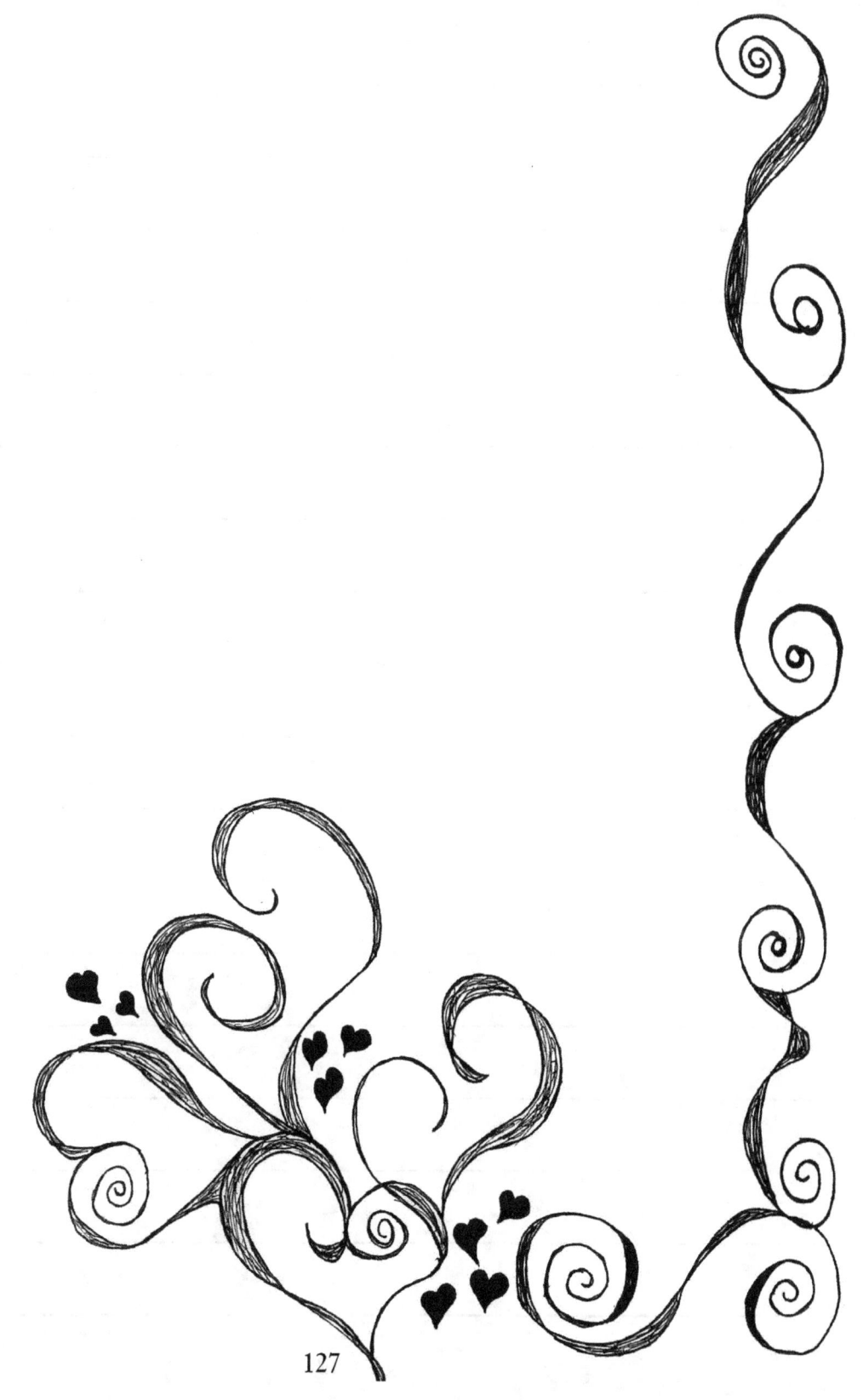

Prefer et obdura

Dolor hic tibi

proderit olim~

Be patient and tough,

Someday this pain

will be useful to you.

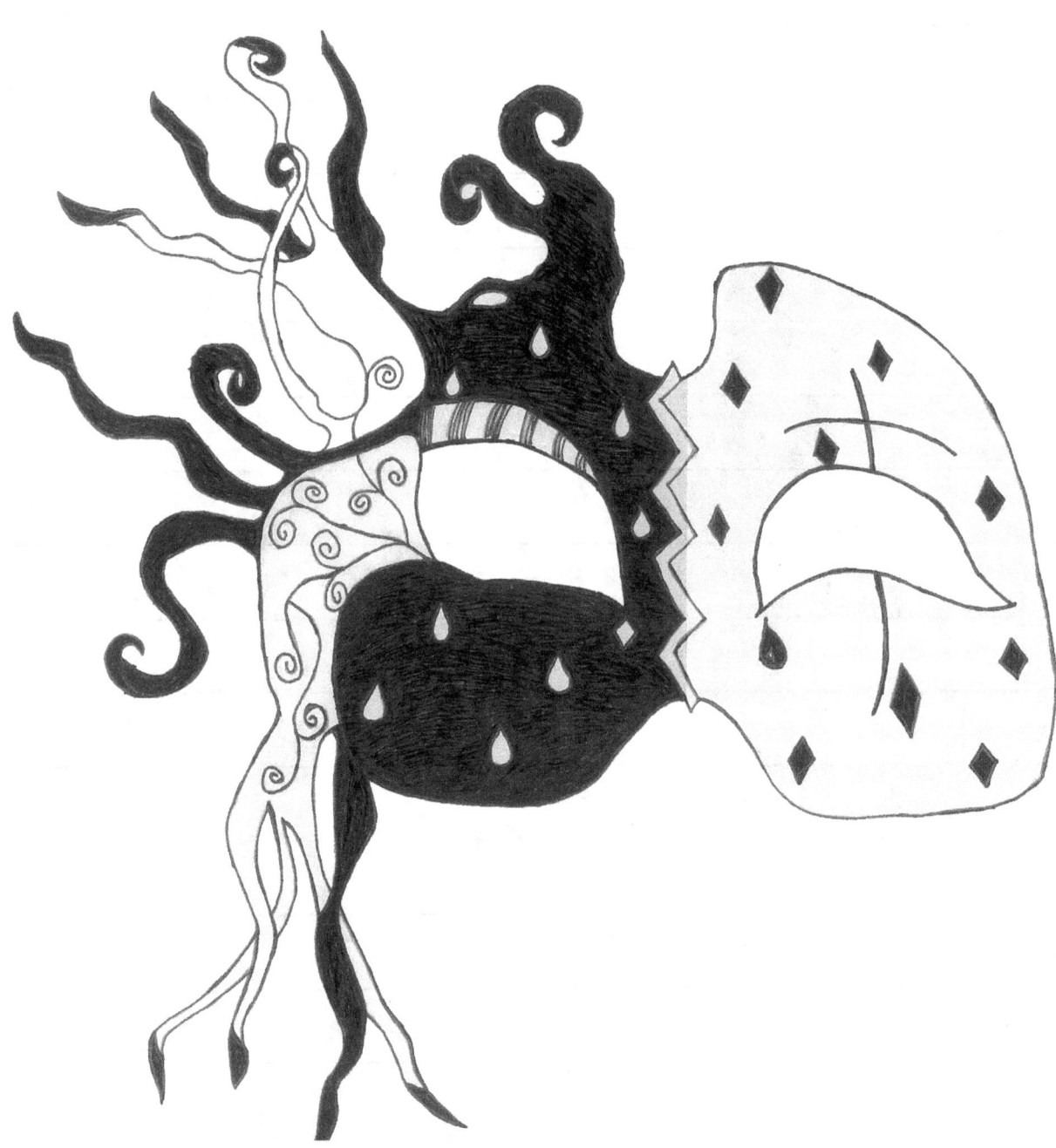

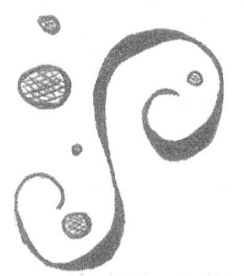
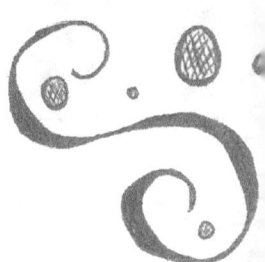

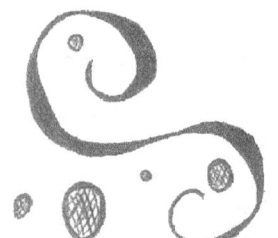
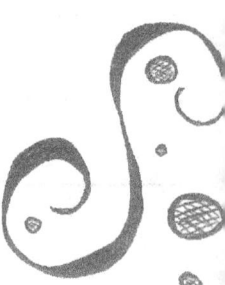

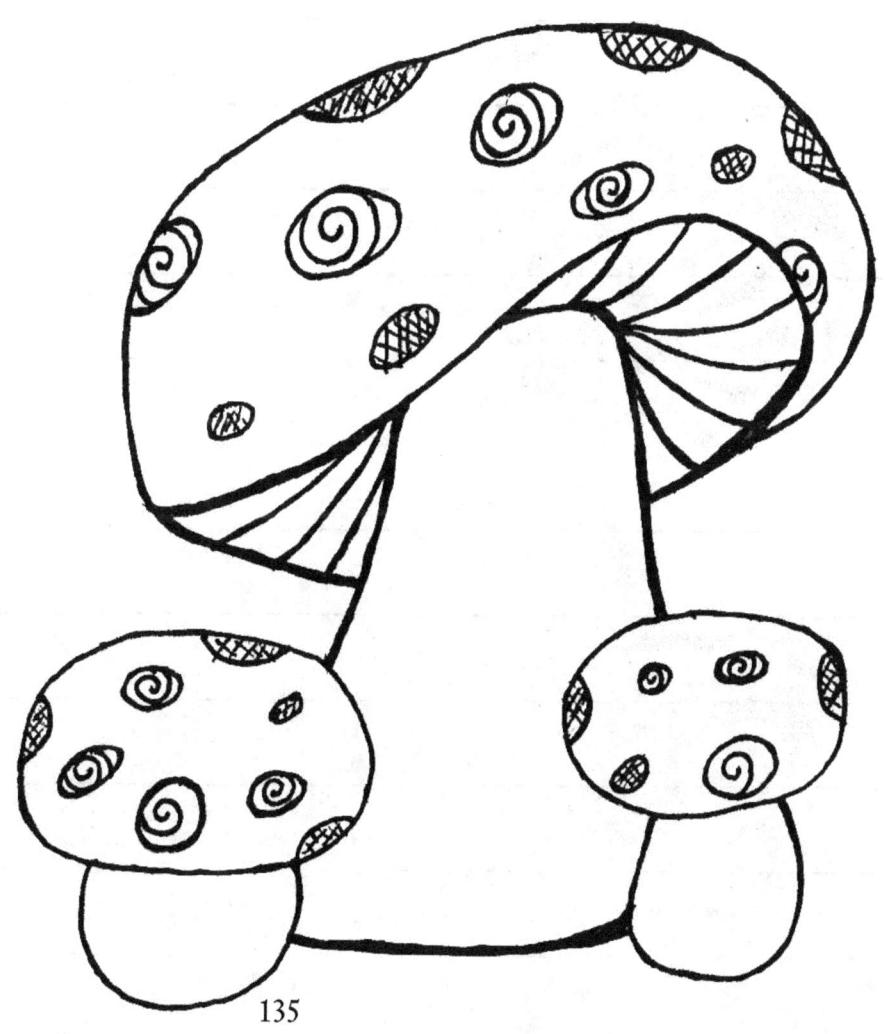

135

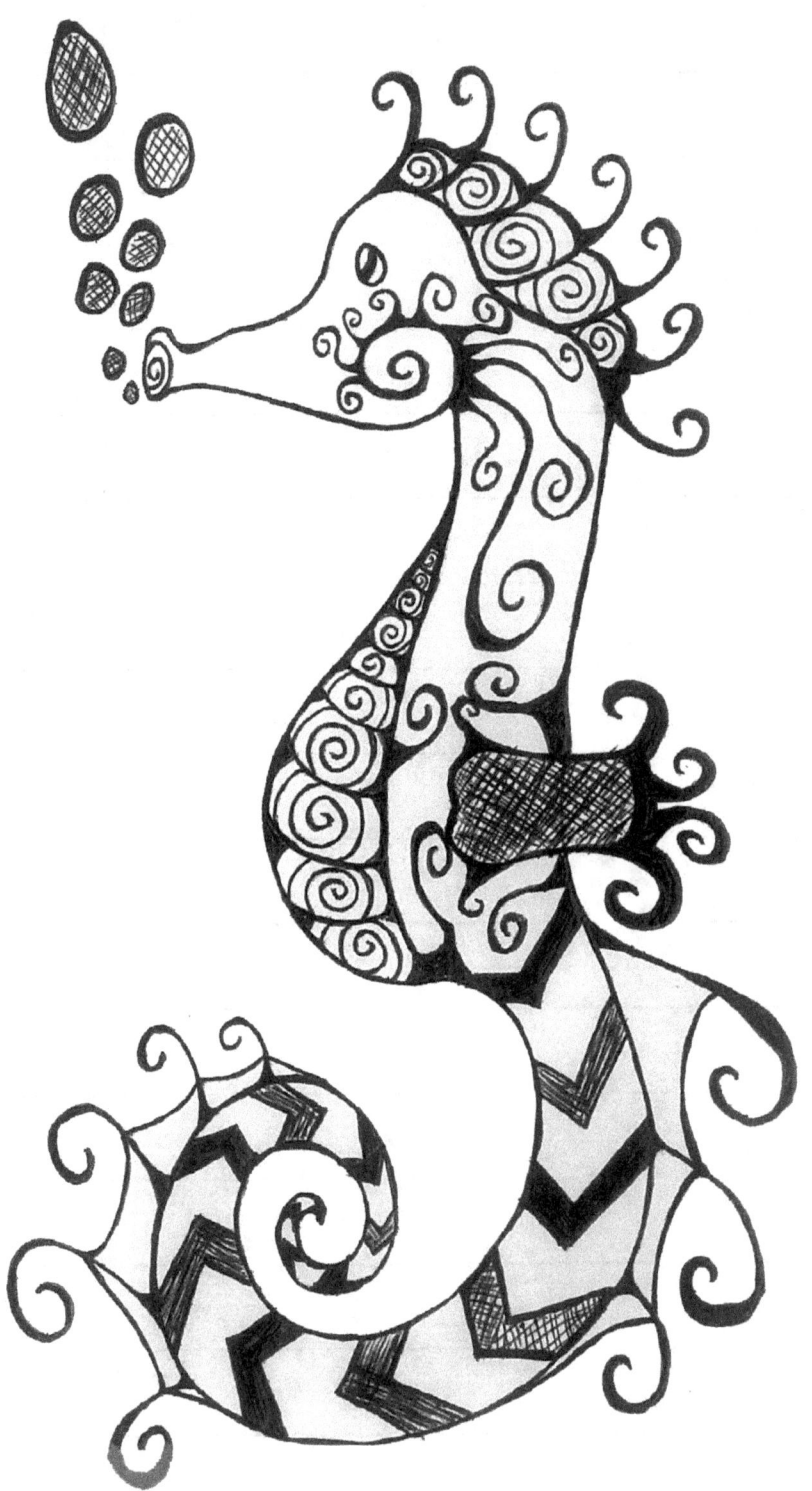

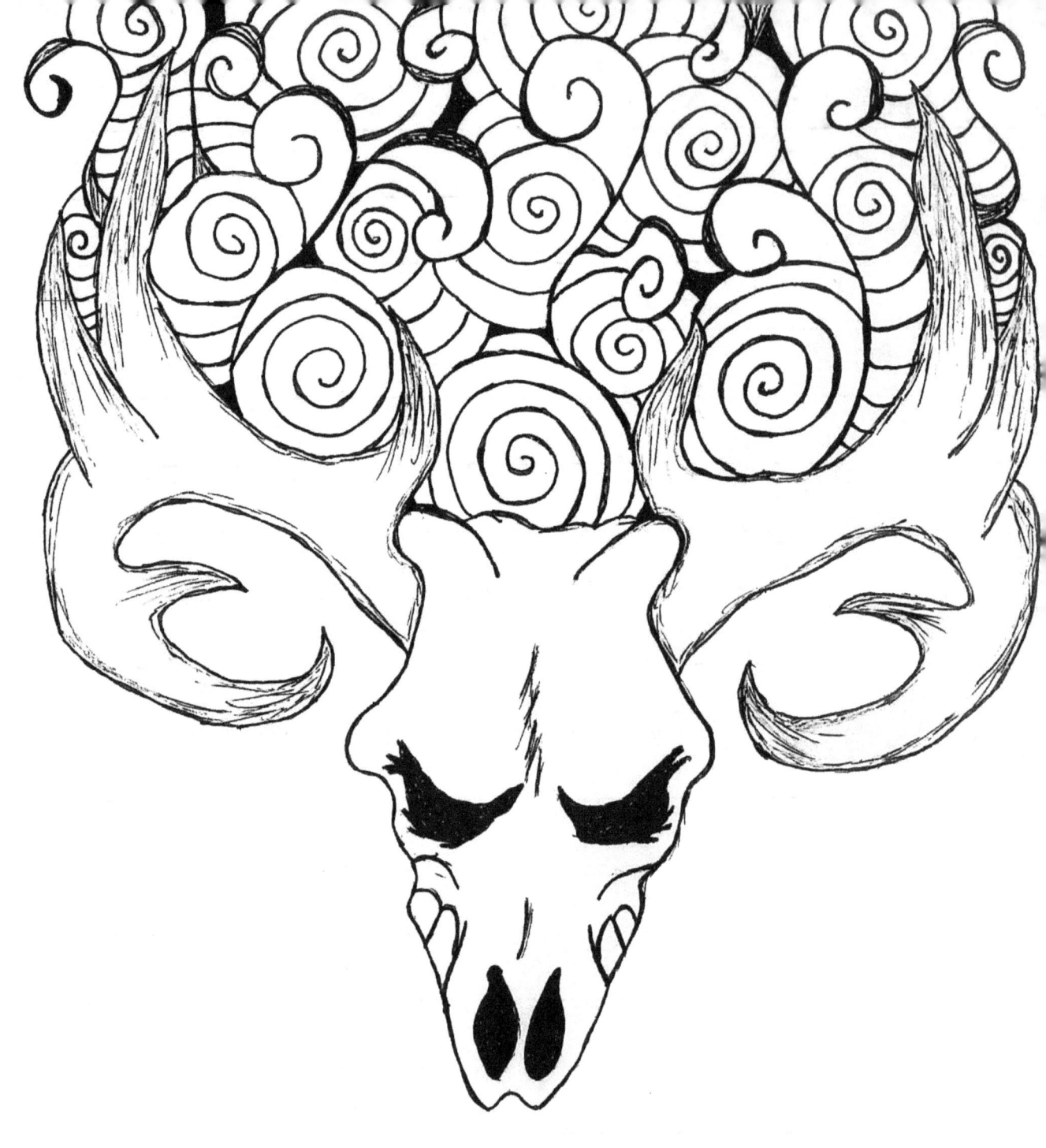

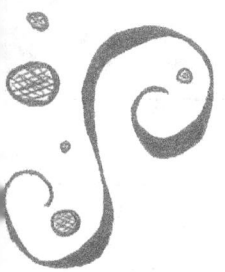
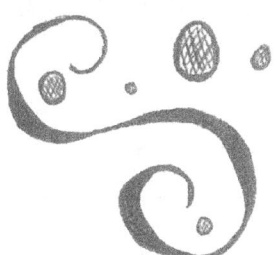
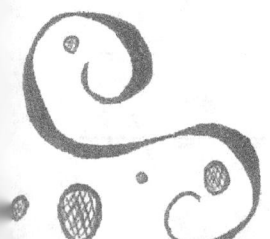
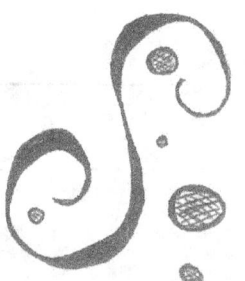

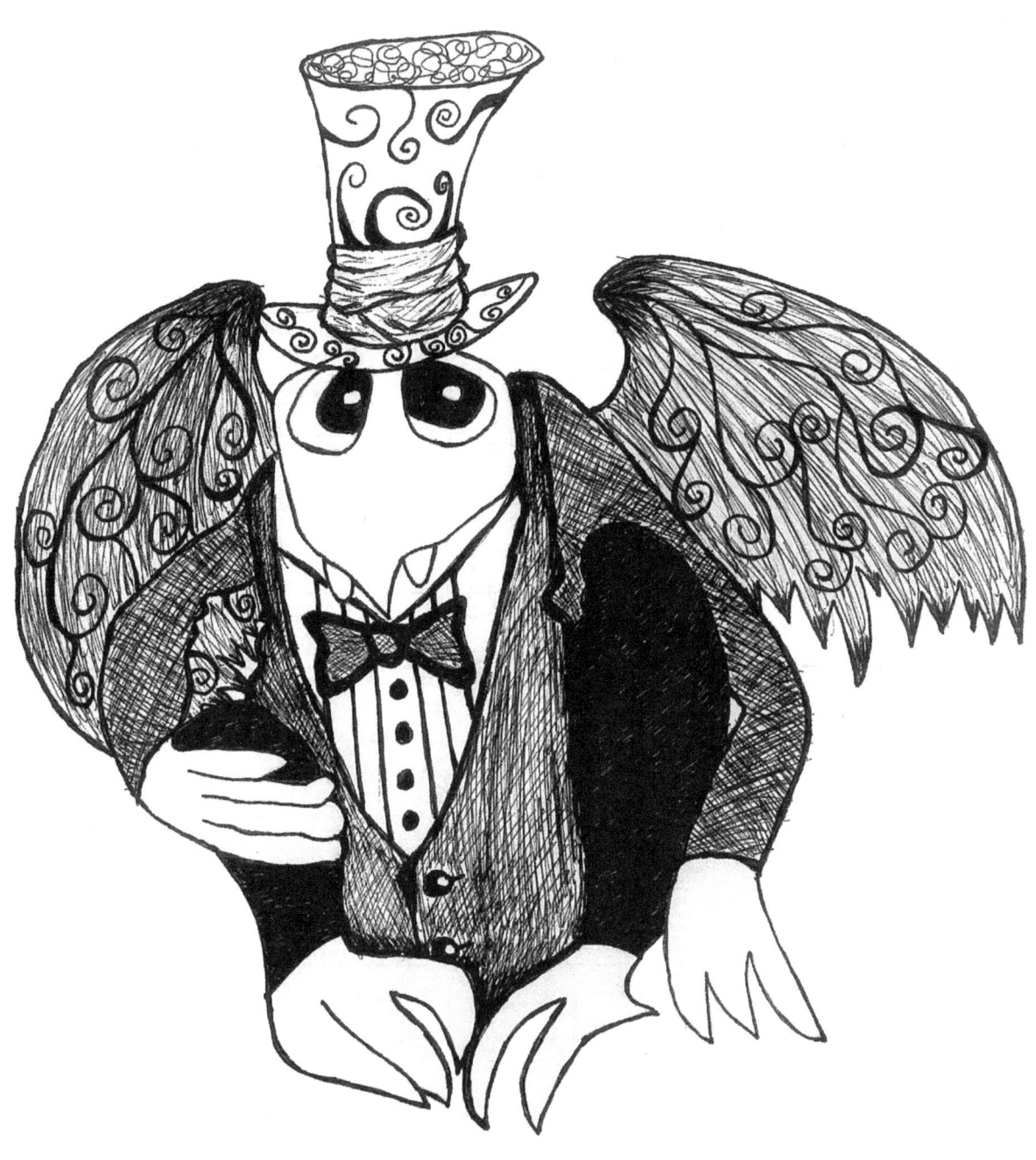

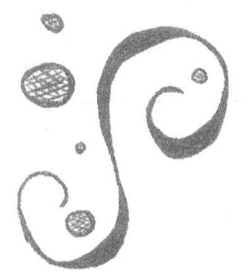
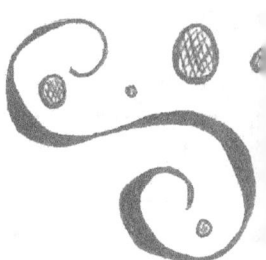

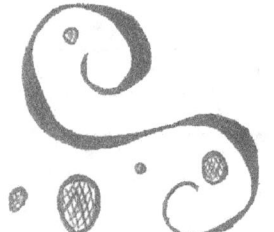
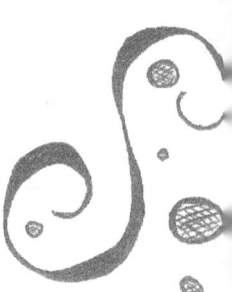

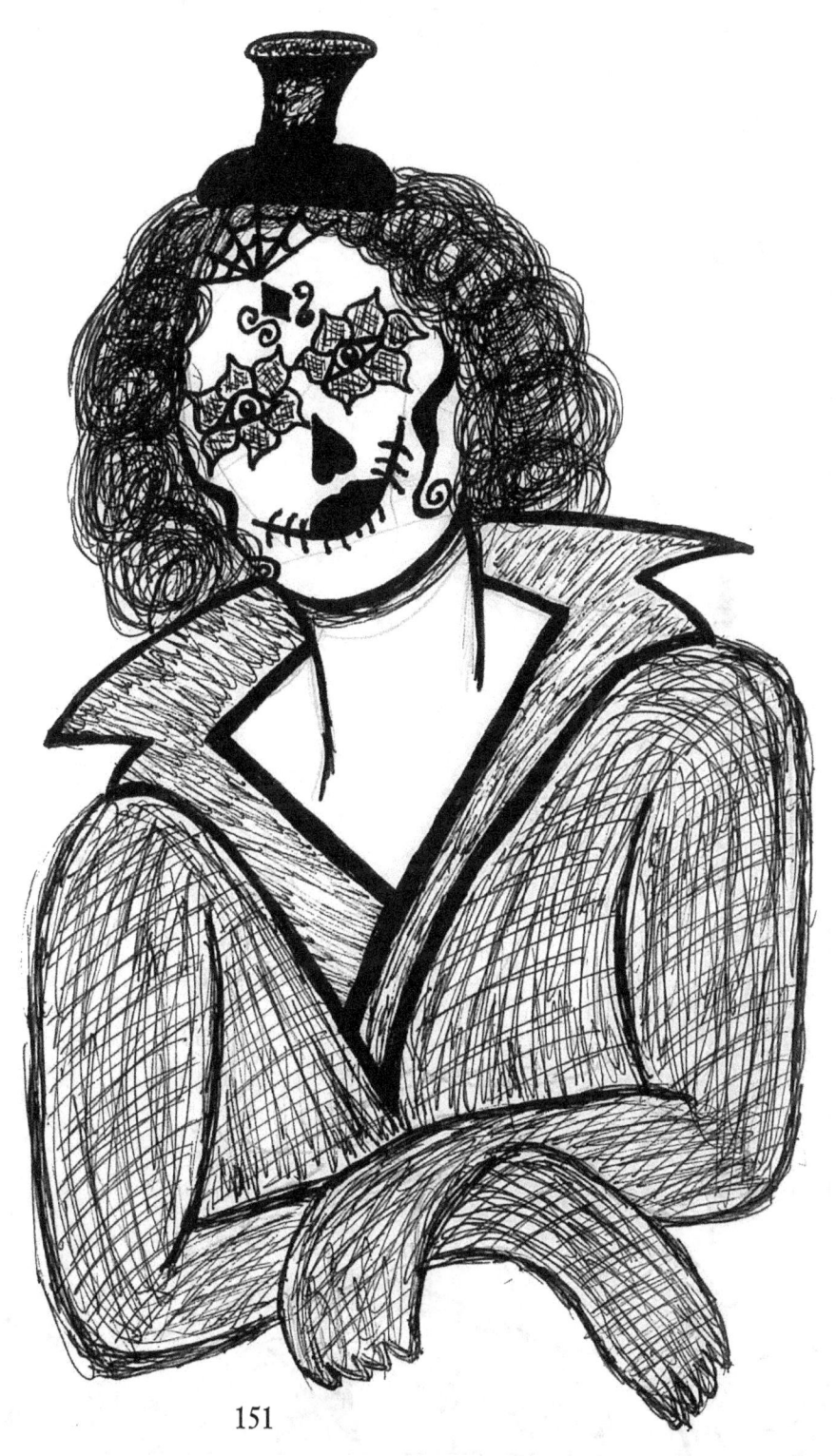

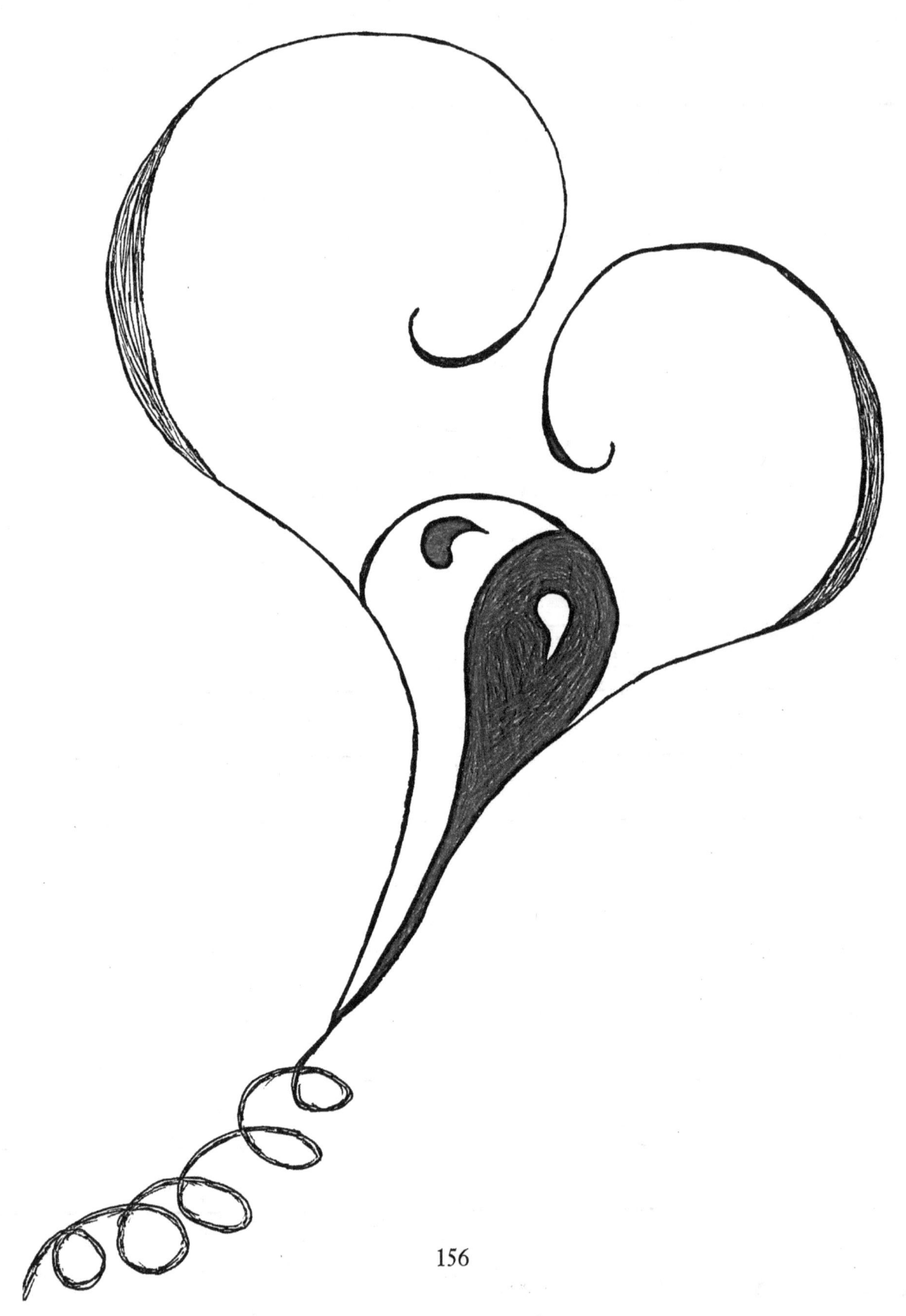

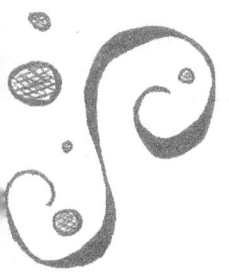
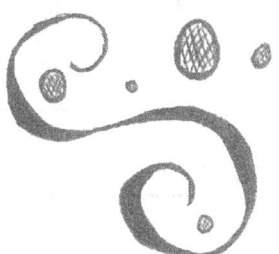

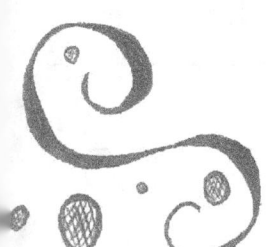
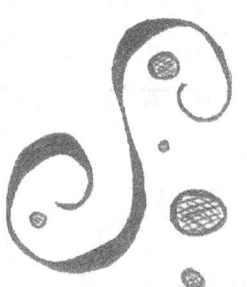

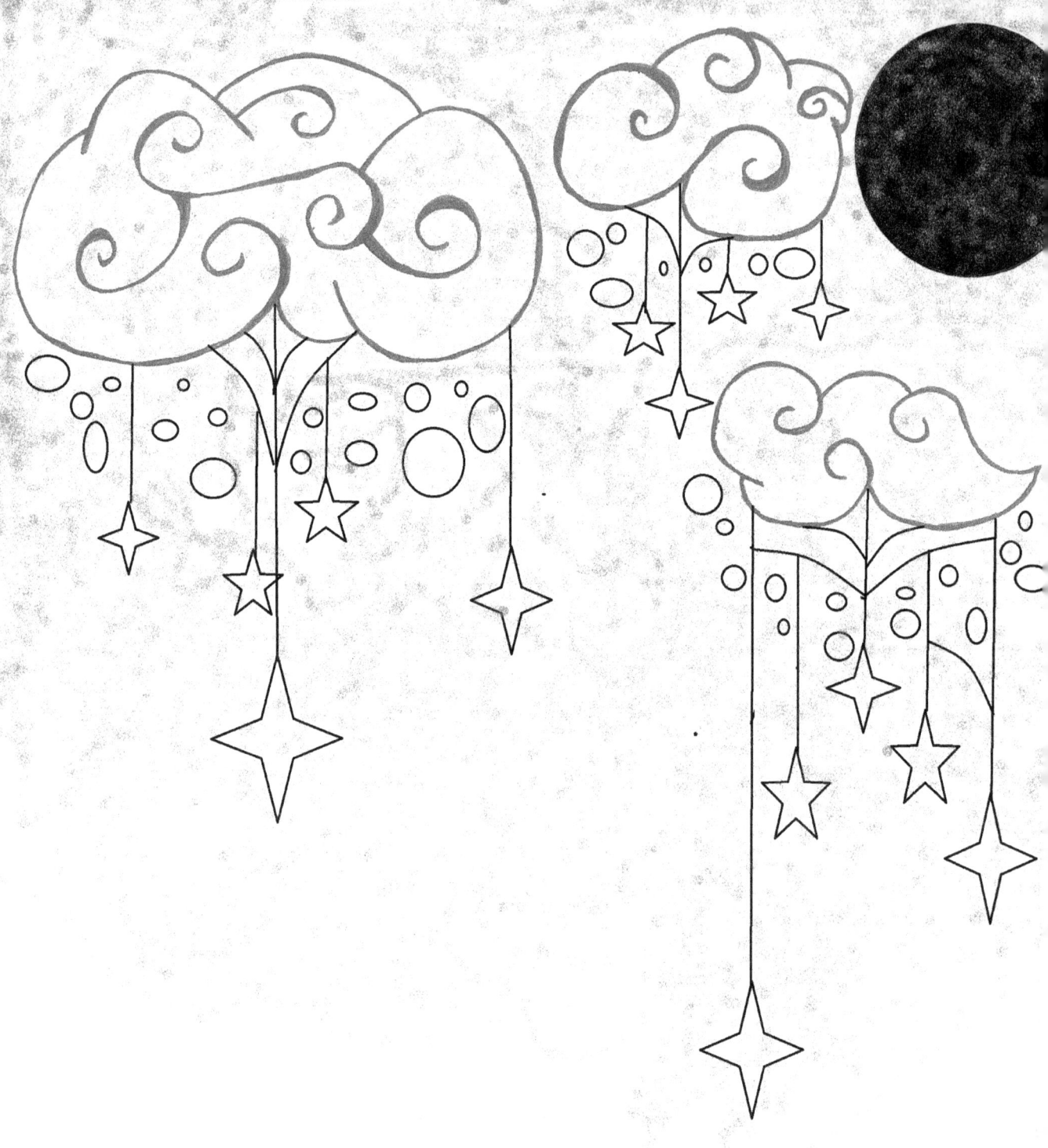

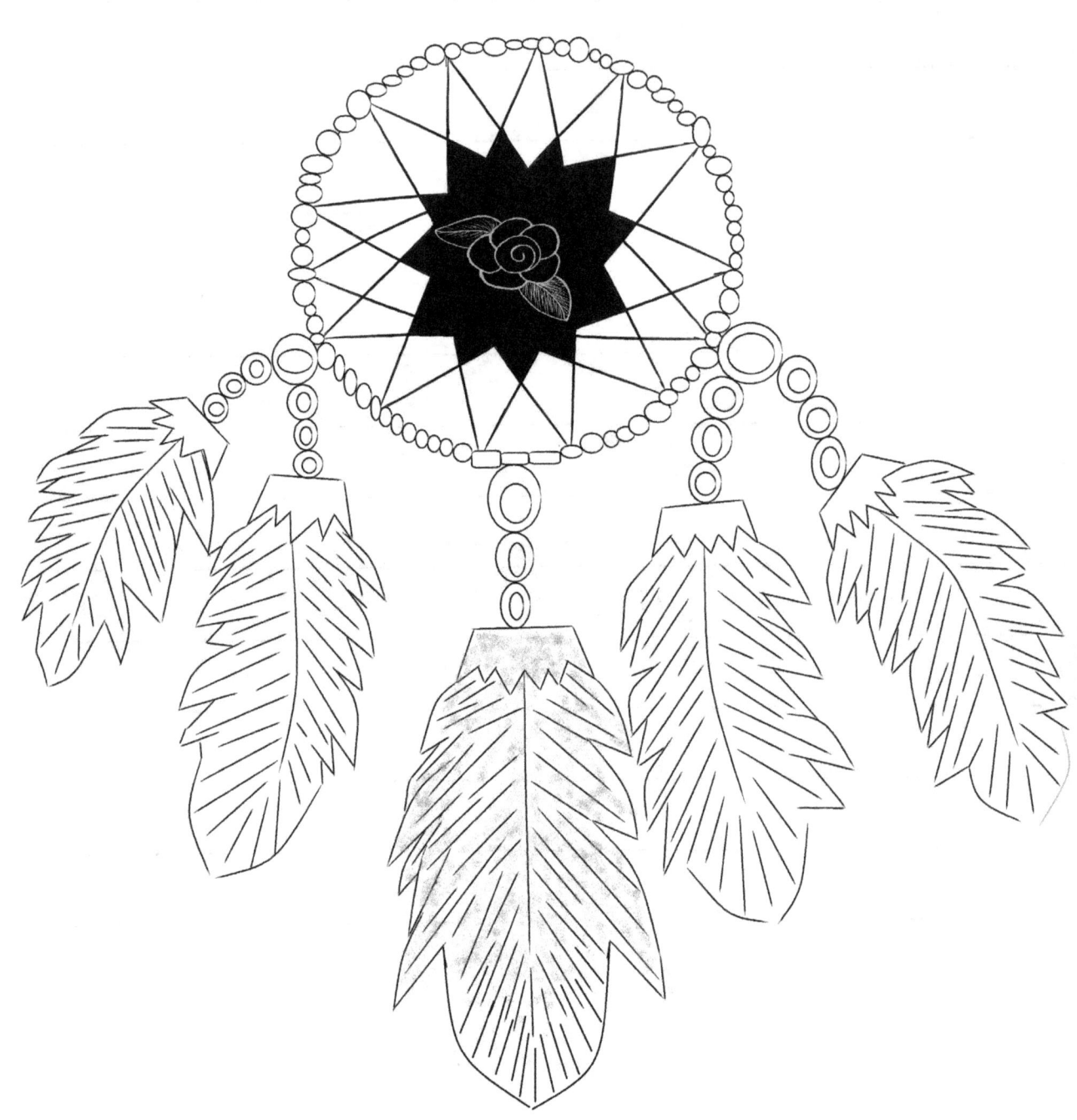

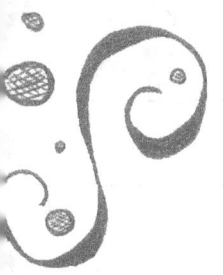
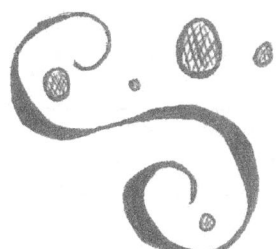

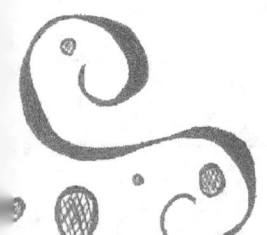
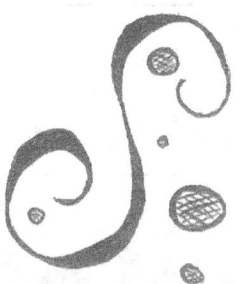

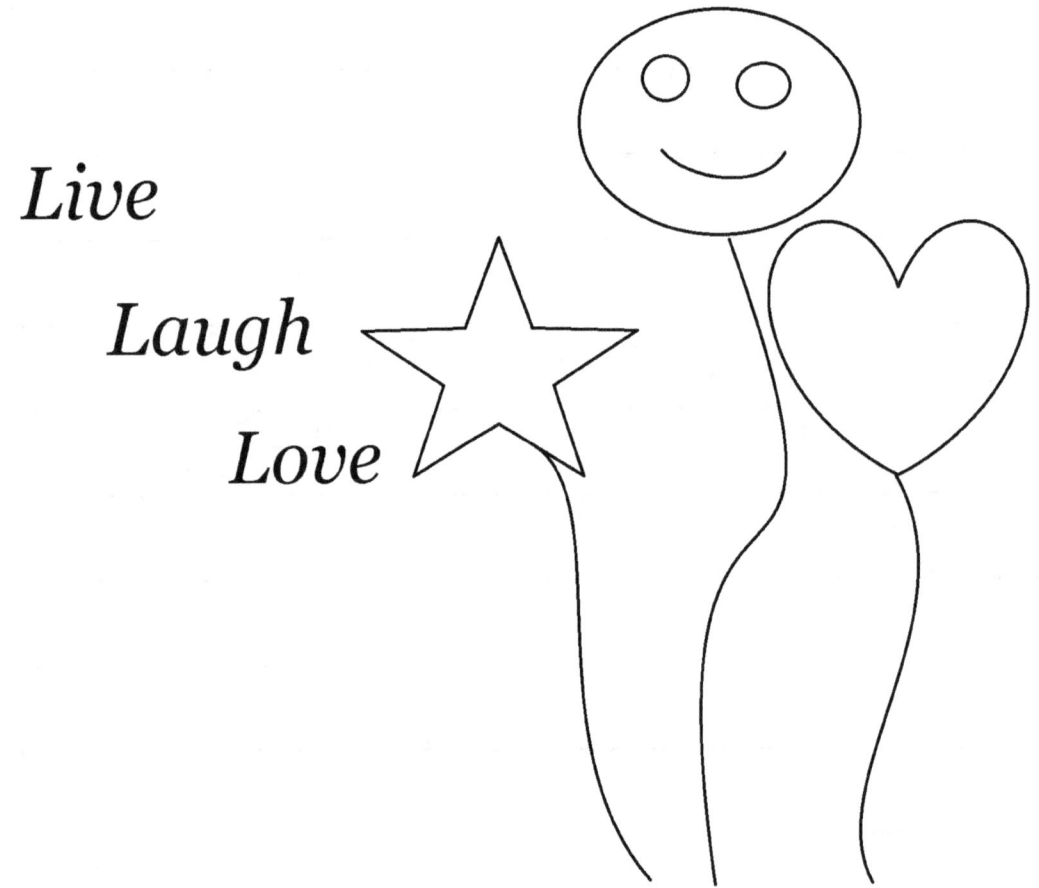

Live

Laugh

Love

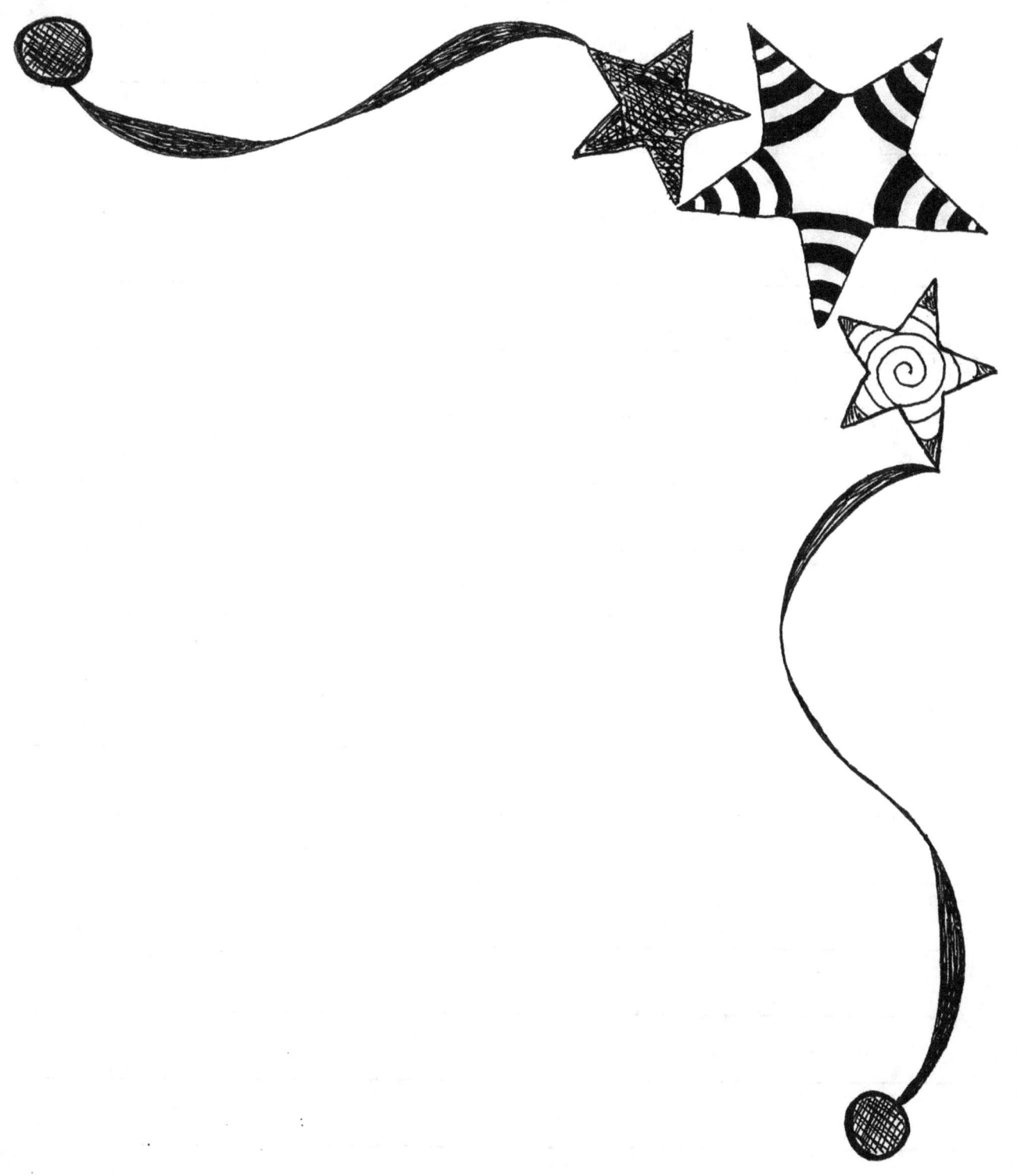

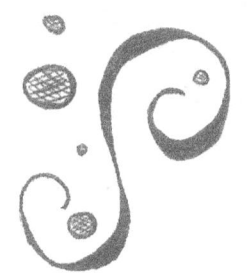
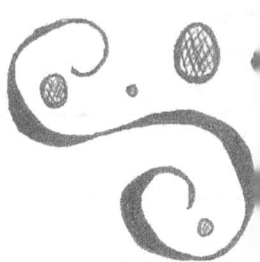

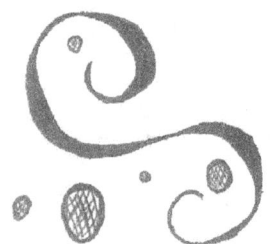
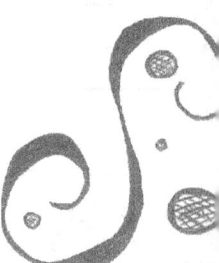

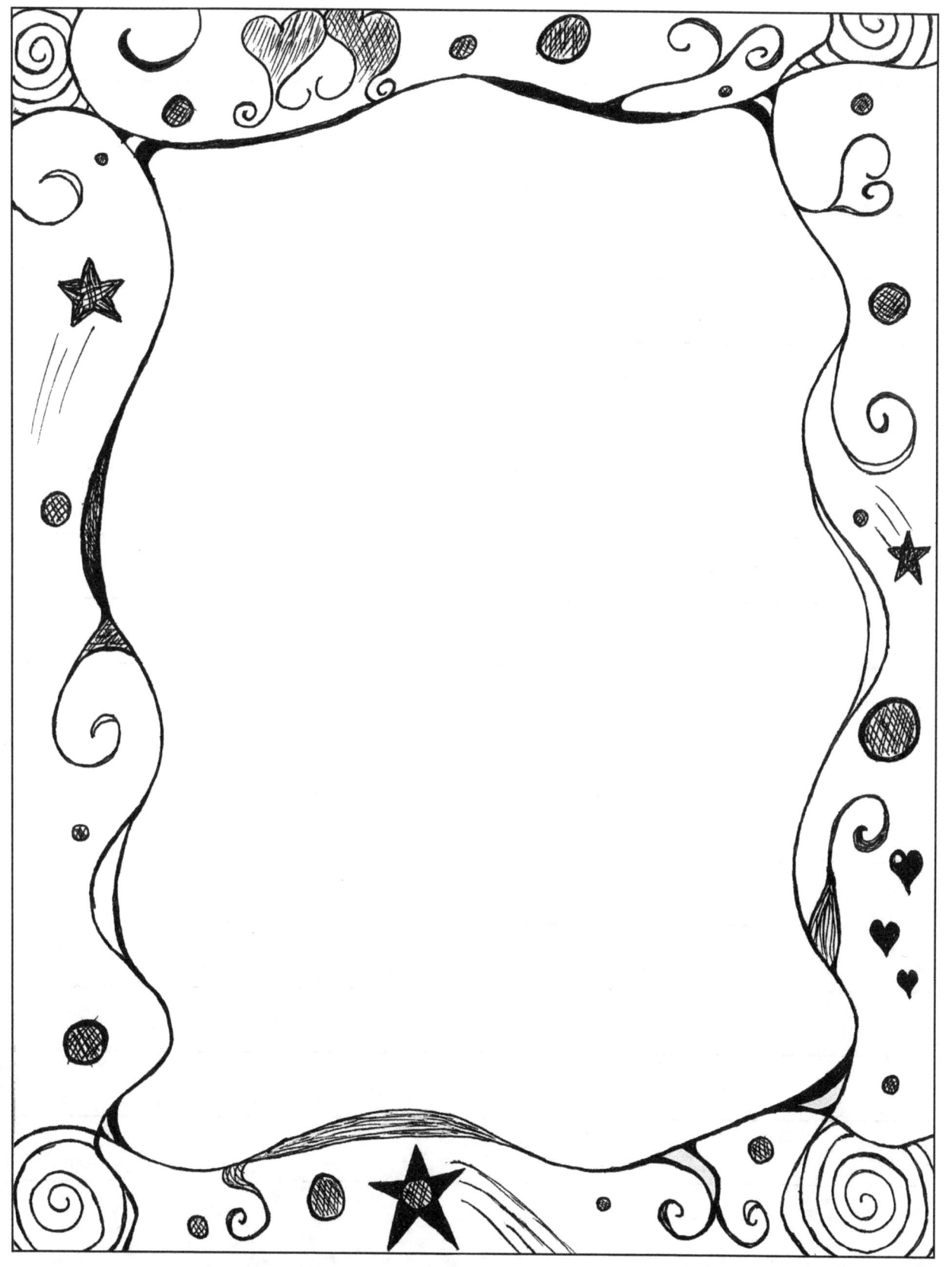

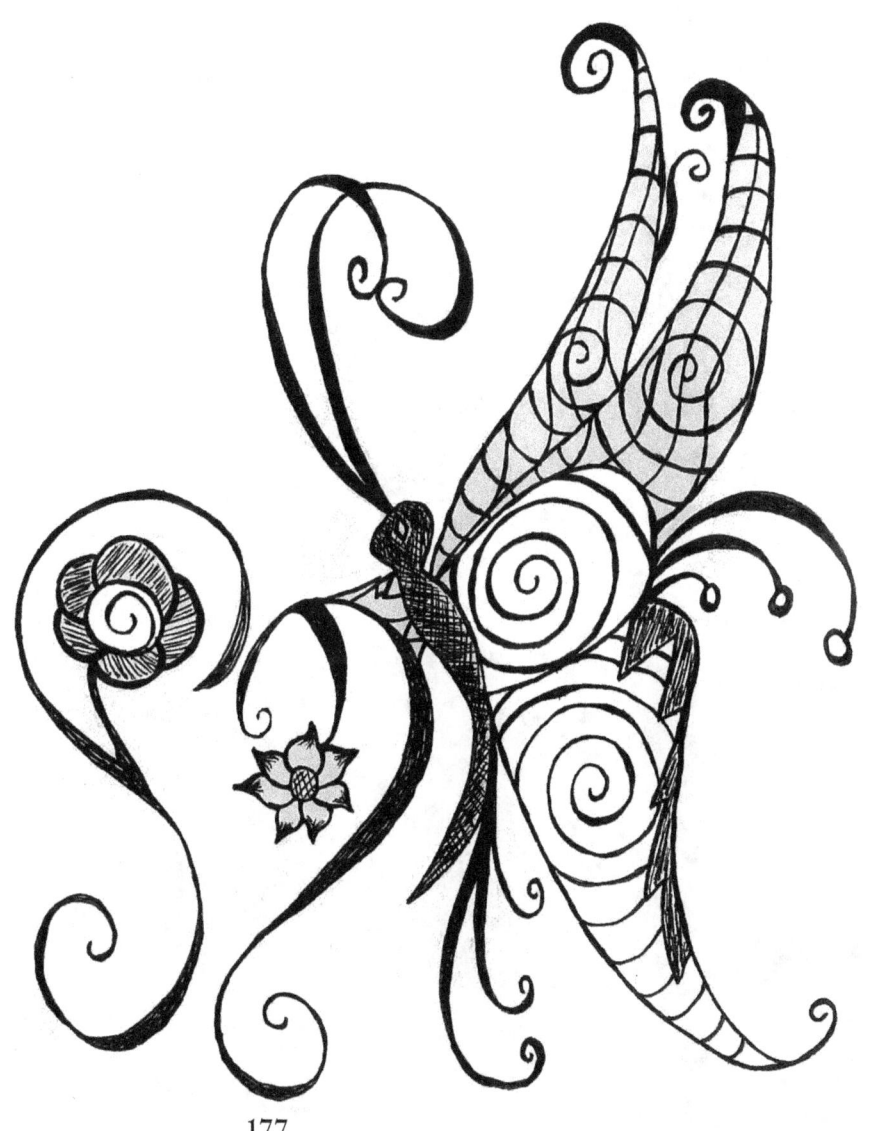

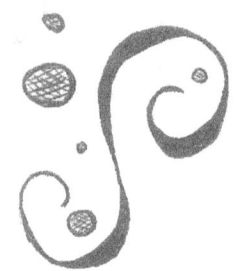
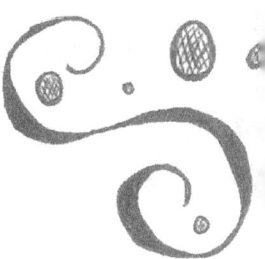

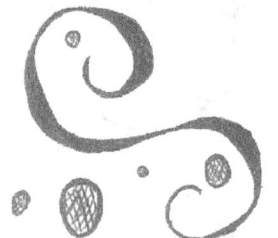
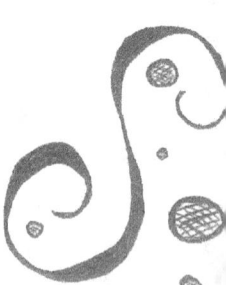

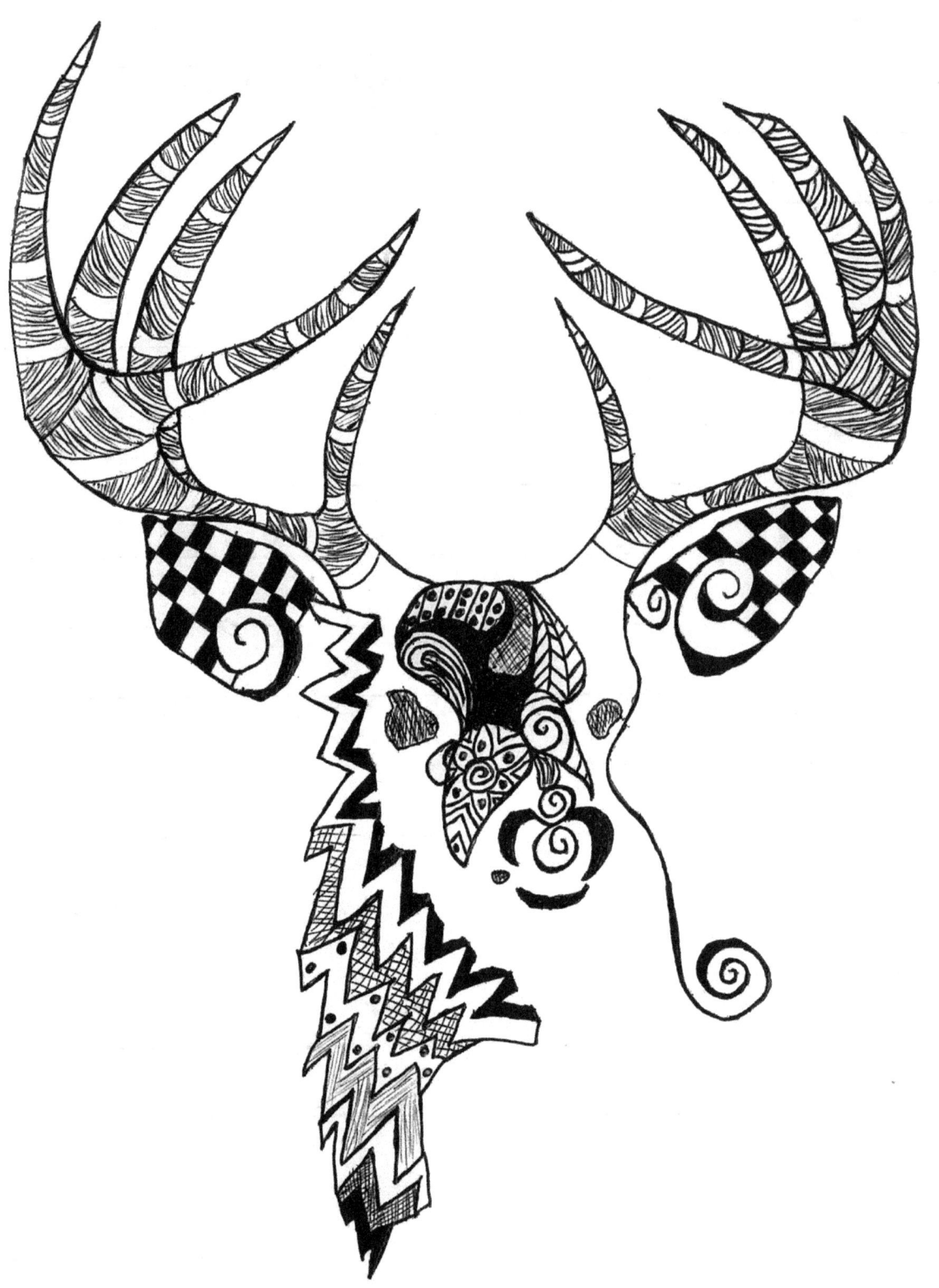

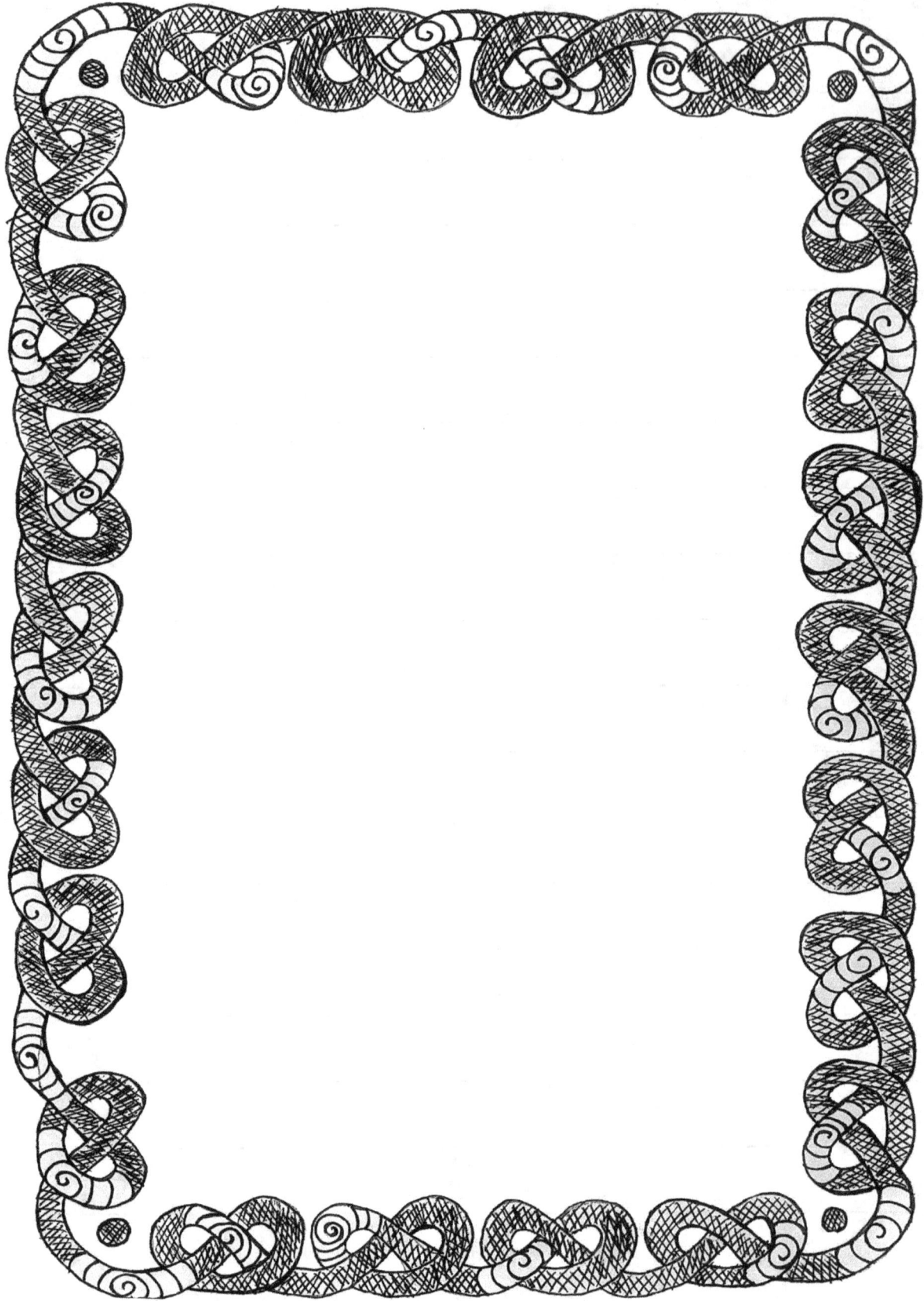

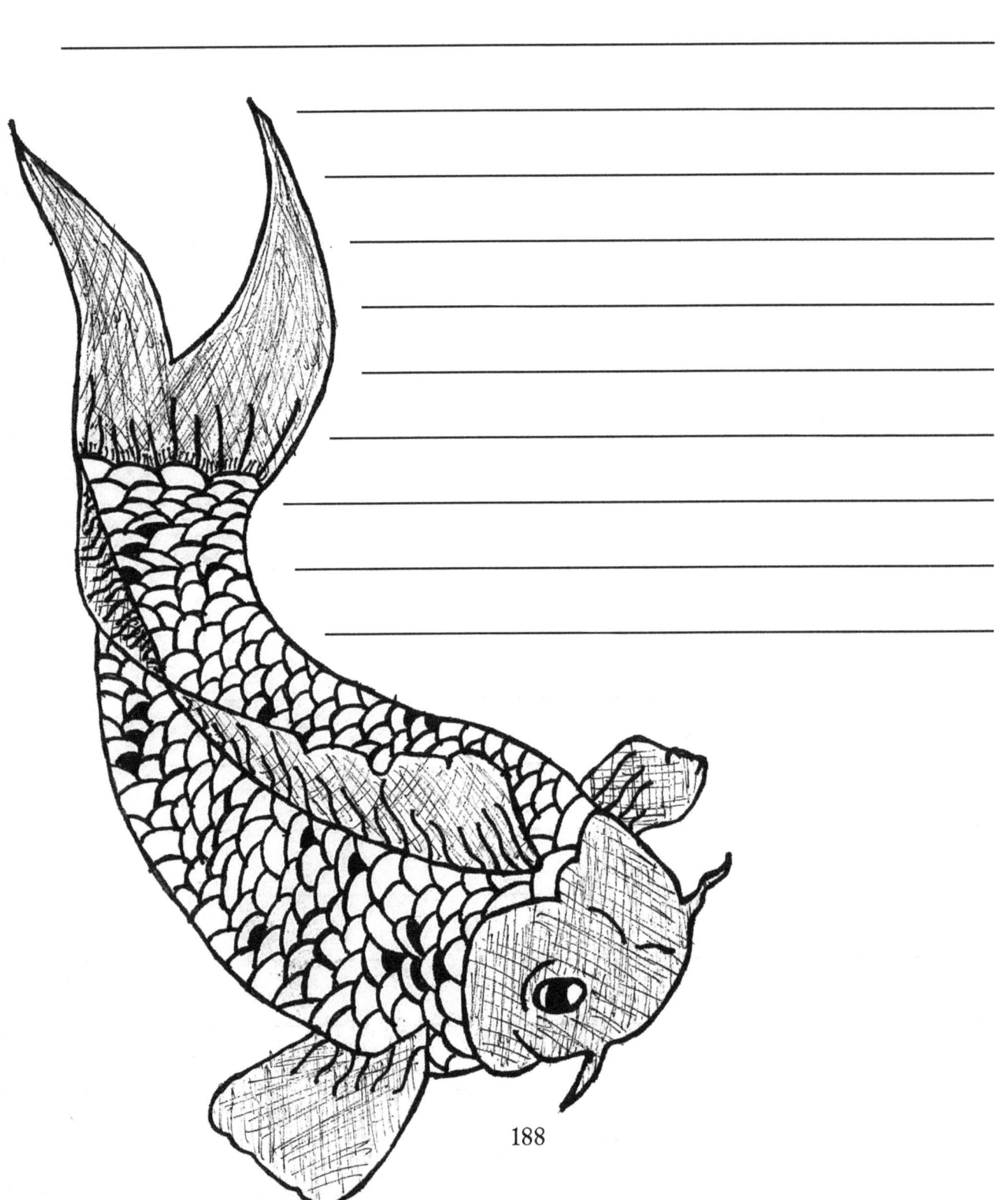

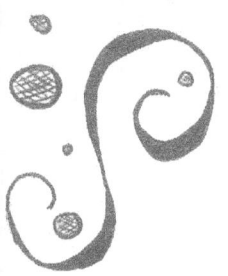
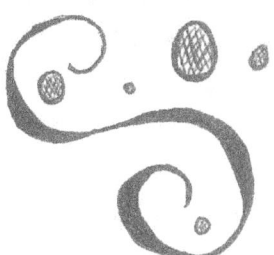
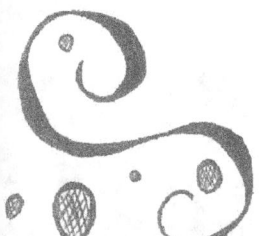
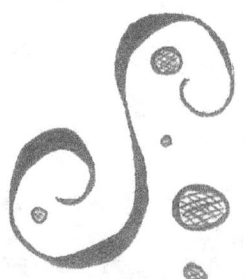

The earth has music for those who listen.

~*Shakespeare*

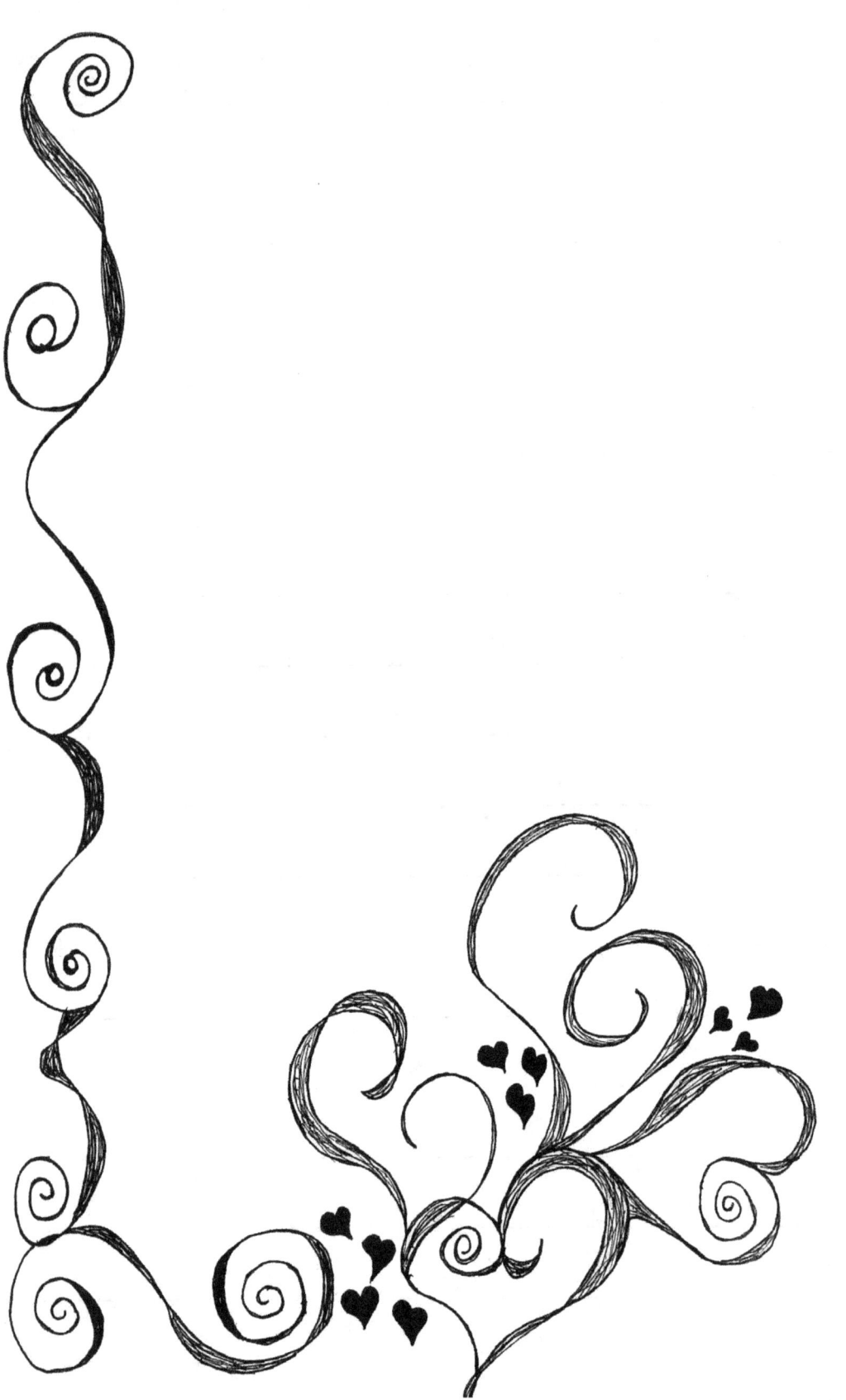

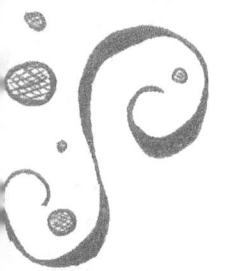
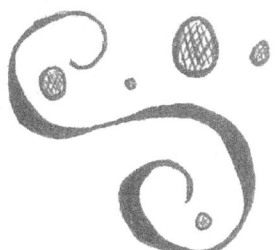

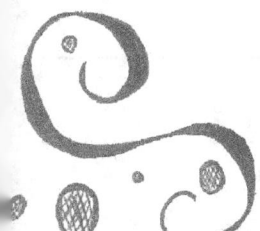
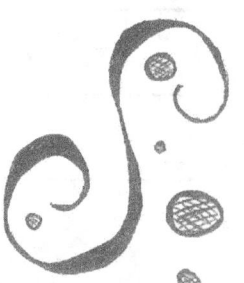